CONCISE HISTORY OF ISRAEL

CONCISE
HISTORY OF ISRAEL

FROM ABRAHAM TO THE BAR
COCHBA REBELLION

by

M. A. BEEK
(*University of Amsterdam*)

Translated by
Arnold J. Pomerans

HARPER & ROW, PUBLISHERS
New York and Evanston

~~933~~
~~B414~~

First published in Holland by W. de Hann under the title
Geschiedenis Van Israël,
this book is published in Great Britain under the title,
A Short History of Israel.

Library of Congress Catalog Card Number: 64-10748

CONTENTS

NOV 3 1967

Contents

LIST OF ILLUSTRATIONS

following pages 64 and 128

vii

List of Illustrations

The Tigris

The temple-gates of Asshur

Assyrian bas-relief being dug out from the ruins of Nimrud (Calah)

Ostracon from Lachish, from the time of Nebuchadnezzar's campaigns

Elephantine papyrus (*c.* 495 B.C.)

The Nabatean royal tombs in Petra[1]

Fragments of the walls of Jerusalem in the Russian Church

Imperial statue, discovered in Caesarea in 1951

Walls of Herod's palace in Jericho

The Sea of Galilee near Capernaum[1]

The Wailing Wall of Jerusalem[1]

The Sea of Galilee seen from the north[1]

Decoration from the Capernaum synagogue (2nd cent. A.D.)[1]

Entrance to the Royal Tombs in Jerusalem[1]

A letter of Bar Cochba

Letter written during the Bar Cochba rebellion

Coins minted during the first and second wars against Rome

ACKNOWLEDGEMENTS

[1] Photographs supplied by M. E. A. ZWIEBERG-WALLER

[2] Photographs supplied by KEREN HAYESOD

THE MAPS

ABBREVIATIONS IN FOOTNOTES

ANEP   *The Ancient Near East in Pictures relating to the Old Testament*, by J. B. Pritchard, Princeton, 1954.

ANET   *Ancient Near Eastern Texts relating to the Old Testament*, by J. B. Pritchard, Princeton, 1955.

BA   *The Biblical Archaeologist.*

BASOR   *Bulletin of the American School of Oriental Research.*

GI   M. Noth: *Geschichte Israels*, Göttingen, 1959 (4th ed.).

JSS   Journal of Semitic Studies.

KS   A. Alt: *Kleine Schriften zur Geschichte des Volkes Israel* (3 vols.), Munich, 1953–1959.

OTS   *Oudtestamentische Studien*, ed. by P. A. H. de Boer (12 vols.), Leyden, 1942–1956.

WGL   E. Auerbach: *Wüste und Gelobtes Land* (2 vols.), Berlin, 1936.

ZDPV   *Zeitschrift des deutschen Palästinavereins.*

INTRODUCTION

Though a history of Israel in Biblical times is far more than a retelling of the Bible in a manner suited to various age-groups or interests, the Old Testament must remain the historian's main source book. He can also consult archaeological discoveries and extra-Biblical texts, but their importance is far less than that of the historical data he can cull from the Bible itself. For while these texts throw a great deal of light on the history of the near east as such, their relevance to the history of Israel has far too often been exaggerated. They keep silent on the most important questions, and where they speak they raise hosts of extraneous problems. In short, they cannot tell us decisively whether or not the Bible is "right."[1]

But when we consult the Old Testament itself, we come up against a formidable obstacle: the Old Testament was not written as a history of Israel's deeds and beliefs, but as a history of God's interventions in that history. Just as the Gospels fail to provide material for the full reconstruction of the life of Jesus, so the Old Testament fails to provide a comprehensive account of the historical events it relates.

Historians study human relationships in the political, social and economic fields. God's historical acts fall outside

[1] For a comprehensive presentation of the relevant archaeological findings, cf. G. E. Wright: *Biblical Archaeology*, Philadelphia–London, 1957. Archaeological material is also incorporated into G. Ricciotti: *The History of Israel*, Milwaukee, 1955. See also H. Michaud: *Sur la pierre et l'argile*, Neuchâtel–Paris, 1957.

their frame of reference, for even those scholars who hold that all history (and not only the history of Israel) is directed by a higher power will nevertheless refrain from explaining historical events as direct acts of God. They must guard against letting their religious convictions colour their purely historical findings, lest they mistake their own fallible judgement for the expression of God's omniscience. Thus the historian may be likened to G. K. Chesterton's police inspector who, when told by a blacksmith accused of murder that God Himself had stricken the victim with the hammer of His wrath, rejoined: "That agent is outside my jurisdiction." The historian must leave the discussion of God's effects on history to the theologian or the philosopher.

Yet the Bible, and particularly such poetic books as Job and the Psalms, describe all historical events in terms of God's will. Throughout the Old Testament, the destiny of Israel is shown to be constantly shaped by the hands of the Almighty—*Elohim* or *Yahweh*—and this interpretation places the modern historian in a great quandary. Even when, like the author of this book, he is convinced of the real presence of the hand of God in these events, he must still write his history of Israel in non-theological terms. At the same time, he must bear in mind that such an account does not represent the full reality.

It has been said that Israel is the first people to have written history. Yet the Israelites wrote history simply to record God's great acts of mercy and salvation. Their history was a source not only of solace but also of promise for the future. All histories which neglect this fact are mere recitals of apparently unconnected data.[1] Thus a history of Israel

[1] Cf. John Bright: *Early Israel in Recent History Writing. Studies in Biblical Theology*, 19, London, 1956.

which dismisses the faith of the prophets simply because the writer considers that faith to have been irrational, is almost inconceivable, and, in any case, completely unimportant. Psalm 78 may perhaps offend against learned scruples when it represents history purely and simply as the proclamation of God's deeds, and yet it accurately paints the background of Israel's historical canvas.

Another problem dogging the steps of the Biblical historian arises from discrepancies in the Biblical sources.[1] However, discussion of these discrepancies often leads to important historical conclusions. For instance, 1 and 2 Kings contain fragments of "annals" which are generally held to give reliable information. These fragments are woven into quite a different type of literature, illustrated by 2 Kings 8 : 4, where the King of Israel asks Gehazi to tell him "all the great things Elisha has done." In the course of his reply, Gehazi outlines the feats of the prophets which form so large a part of the Books of Kings, and weaves a legend differing in style and content from the purely descriptive passages. Then there is yet a third kind of historical writing, intended for public recitation during religious or national festivals, and embellished accordingly.[2] Here, the hero is usually turned into a king and his deeds are fitted into a classical pattern. The "king" himself is never named; at best he is given a genealogical title, viz. Ben-hadad (son of Hadad) in 2 Kings 6 : 24. Such references are of little help to the historian.

---

[1] For an analysis of the sources, cf. M. Noth: *Ueberlieferungsgeschichtliche Studien* I, 1943, and *Ueberlieferungsgeschichte des Pentateuchs*, Stuttgart, 1948.

[2] 2 Chron. 12 : 15 states that the acts of Rehoboam were recorded in the book of Shemaiah the prophet and of Iddo the seer. There thus was a prophetic type of historical narration.

Still more complicated is the problem of assessing the historical reliability of Biblical stories connected with high festivals. The exodus of Israel from Egypt is a classical case in point, since, in reconstructing this event which the Jews commemorate and relive annually as the Passover, twentieth-century historians wishing to know what precisely happened and when, sift and arrange the material until they arrive at an explanation which, ignoring miracles and divine guidance, conforms with what is considered the rational view of the matter.[1] In fact, while the sources give no reason to doubt the historicity of the events themselves, they suggest that the question of how precisely those events occurred may never receive a satisfactory answer.

The most difficult problem of all is to arrive at conclusions about the traditional accounts of the period before Moses, for while the sources are strikingly unanimous about the existence of this nomadic or pre-nomadic period, the story of the Patriarchs is written in a manner that prevents us from making any sort of really convincing reconstruction.

I fully realise that a history of Israel must be based on the detailed investigation of all the available sources. This is precisely what Alt and Noth have done so impressively. However, such detailed investigations inevitably run the danger of leading to too schematic a conception of the origins of the Biblical tradition, and while this conception may fulfil the demands of western scholarship, it fails to do justice to life itself. The oral and written traditions of peasants of nomadic origin must have been far too complex to have followed a logical pattern. Hence I am convinced that every

---

[1] Cf. J. Pedersen: *Israel*, III–IV, Copenhagen–London, 1940, additional note I: The Crossing of the Red Sea and the Paschal Legend, pp. 728–737.

Biblical reference must be tested individually not only for its agreement with archaeological findings, but also for its inherent worth. The purely historical method (e.g. of Alt and Noth) is far too sceptical to provide any kind of history of Israel before Joshua's time. Thus, while Noth's *History of Israel* displays a great deal of sound critical sense, he forgets that critical sense must also be turned against too much speculation, e.g. such a claim as that all Biblical accounts of the Patriarchs were altered beyond recognition by later generations.

A critical examination of the available sources is the prerequisite of all historical research, particularly when it is research into the history of God's chosen people. Only a critical approach can preserve us from the opposite error of considering all Biblical accounts true beyond all doubt and of trying to make them all agree with one another. This is a pitfall which Y. Kaufmann's *The Biblical Account of the Conquest of Palestine* (Jerusalem, 1953) does not escape altogether, for while the author rightly attacks the literary method of Alt and Noth, he goes too far when he declares the story of Joshua a historical fact, thus detracting from the value of his general argument. The result is a description of a military campaign more reminiscent of a *Blitzkrieg* under a brilliant general than of the invasion of a civilised country by nomadic tribes.[1]

Having explained the problems involved, we can now present our own attempt to write a history of Israel, based on the most up-to-date historical findings.[2] The reader is

[1] Cf. John Bright: *op. cit.*, pp. 72–74.

[2] A related attempt was made in E. L. Ehrlich: *Geschichte Israels von den Anfängen bis zur Zerstörung des Tempels*, Berlin, 1958. For a more detailed history of a portion of the story covered in this book see *History of Israel* by John Bright, Philadelphia, 1959.

warned that all he will be given is a historical outline. It goes without saying that the religious beliefs which helped to shape Israel's history will not be completely ignored, but, for practical reasons, these beliefs can only be treated fully in a special work. For, when all is said and done, it is not really as important to stress the religious factor in the history of Israel, as to join in the hymn of praise to God which that history so persuasively sings.

I

THE SETTING

THE most important part of Biblical history took place in Palestine.[1] The name "Palestine" first occurs in Herodotus (VII, 89), and is derived from "Philistine" (The Philistine country). The Israelites called the people who lived in the southern coastal plain *Pelishtim*—"Philistines." In A.D. 135, Palestine became a Roman province under that name. The Old Testament itself calls the Biblical land *Canaan*, a term that was once thought to have been derived from a Hebrew word meaning "low-lying," but which modern scholars trace back to the Akkadian word for "purple" which occurs in the tablets from Nuzu (fourteenth–fifteenth century B.C.). Since the Greek name for "purple" is *phoenix*, Canaan may have been the O.T. synonym for Phoenicia.

Ever since Palestine was incorporated into the Roman Empire, its borders have kept changing. Under the British mandate, Palestine (excluding Transjordan) covered 10,429 square miles—an area slightly smaller than Belgium. The country is flanked by the Mediterranean in the west and by the desert in the east and the south. In the north it

---

[1] See the *Atlas of the Bible* by Luc. H. Grollenberg, London, 1956; *The Westminster Historical Atlas to the Bible* edited by G. E. Wright and F. V. Filson, Philadelphia, 1956, and *The Rand McNally Bible Atlas*, edited by Emil G. Kraeling, Chicago, 1962.

merges into the mountains of Lebanon. The Old Testament refers to the length of the land (inaccurately) as "from Dan to Beer-sheba"—some 150 miles.

Palestine is cut in two by the River Jordan, which rises in Mount Hermon and flows down to the Dead Sea. On its way, it feeds Lake Huleh and the Sea of Galilee which lies some 650 feet below sea level and which, because of its shape, was called *Chinnereth*, meaning, "zither." The Dead or Salt Sea, lying some 1,300 feet below sea level, is the deepest natural depression on earth. The children of Israel lived on either side of the Jordan. The Arabah, the valley south of the Dead Sea, stretched as far as the Gulf of Aqaba.

The Jordan has carved a deep valley out of the mountains. Near Beth-shan (south of the Sea of Galilee) and Jericho (north of the Dead Sea) this valley widens into a plain. A region on either side of the Jordan, bounded by the Mediterranean in the west and by the desert in the east, is covered by undulating mountains. Thus Jerusalem is roughly 2,500 feet above sea level, while Jericho, which is only some twenty miles away, is 825 feet *below* sea level.

Northern and southern Palestine are divided by Mt. Carmel which runs from the N.W. to the S.E. and projects into the Mediterranean. North of Mt. Carmel lies the fertile plain of Esdraelon, called *Emek* in modern Hebrew. In Biblical times, the coastal strip was inhabited by the Philistines in the south, and by the Phoenicians in the north. At that time, the southern region—now called the Negev—played an important role. Even in Joshua's day, seventeen towns were mentioned in it. Its soil is rich and, by irrigating it with rainwater caught in cisterns, the inhabitants man-

aged to live fairly prosperously until the seventh century
A.D.

In Palestine the rainy season extends from the end of
October to the beginning of April. Jerusalem has an average
of fifty-eight days of rain with a total rainfall of 17 inches.
Most of the rain comes down in January; another "late
rainfall" occurs in the Spring. Failure of rain led to "three-
year droughts" because the preceding and following dry
periods were included (I Kings 18 : 1). Usually, soon after
midday, there is a refreshing wind which is called "the cool
of the day" (Gen. 3 : 8). Another, hot, wind (the *khamsin* in
Arabic), blowing from the desert in the east causes the
"grass to wither and the flower to fade" (Isa. 40 : 7 and
Hos. 13 : 15). The atmosphere becomes particularly stifling
just after the *khamsin* has ceased. According to the Bible,
Jonah was plagued by this very type of desert wind (Jonah
4 : 8).

Palestine is part of the "Fertile Crescent" joining Egypt to
Mesopotamia. It is for this reason that it was called the
land of milk and honey. That phrase, however, could only
have been coined by nomadic tribes in the light of the contrast with the wastes from which they came. Even today, as
we travel along the Scorpion Pass to Beer-sheba and thence
into the mountains of Judea, we are amazed at the change
from barren into rich soil. We can understand how a band of
poor and underfed nomads must have marvelled when they
beheld hillsides covered with vineyards or studded with olive-
fields, and fertile fields, and green pastures. Clearly, at the
time, Palestine was anything but the barren and neglected
country that met the nineteenth-century Zionist pioneers.
When southern Palestine was thickly populated, and when
the Emek and large parts of the coastal plain had not yet

been turned into swamp, it was a "rich and a pleasant land" (Dan. 8 : 9) which aroused the envy not only of roving nomads, but also of the great powers. No wonder then that the geographical situation, the fertility and the economic potential of Palestine had so considerable an influence on the fate and the history of Israel.

II

THE PATRIARCHS

THE Israelites always preserved the memory of their early origins: e.g. on offering the first fruits, they had to recite before the altar: "An Aramaean was my father" (Deut. 26 : 5).[1] We are told that Abraham sent his servant to choose Isaac's wife from among his kinsfolk in *Aram Naharayim* (Gen. 24 : 10), i.e. Aram of the two rivers. The rivers were probably, though not certainly, the Euphrates and the Tigris. (The Hebrew ending -*ayim* represents both the dual of nouns and also geographical place names, e.g. *Jerushalayim*, *Mahanayim*, etc.)[2] According to the rather uncertain tradition of Gen. 11 : 31, the father of Abram (later called Abraham) came from Ur of the Chaldees to Haran (near Carchemish on the Euphrates); Haran also played an important role in the story of Jacob (Israel). In Gen. 15 : 7 we are told that God spoke to Abraham in words reminiscent of the beginning of the Ten Commandments: "I am the Lord that brought thee out of Ur of the Chaldees." This reference simply means that Abraham and his followers came from the *region* of Ur in Southern Mesopotamia, for the Bible leaves no doubt that the Patriarchs were roving nomads and not town-dwellers. Biblical stories about the

[1] M. A. Beek: "Das Problem des aramäischen Stammvaters," *OTS*, VIII, pp. 193–212.

[2] R. T. O'Callaghan: *Aram Naharaim, A Contribution to the History of Upper Mesopotamia in the 2nd Millenium B.C.*, Rome, 1948.

origins of the Israelites are agreed on only one point: the Patriarchs were of Aramaean stock. They are said to have broken away from one of the many tribes that later came together in Damascus.[1]

The family tree in Gen. 11 : 10 ff. supports the N.W. Mesopotamian origin of the patriarchs. Haran, the name of one of Abraham's brothers, was the name of a town which flourished in the nineteenth and eighteenth century B.C. Abraham's other brother was called Nahor, and it was to Nahor that Abraham sent his servant to seek a wife for Isaac (Gen. 24 : 10). The name Nahor also occurs as the place name *Nahuru* in the Mari texts (eighteenth century B.C.) and on later Assyrian clay tablets.[2] Nahor was therefore a town named after a tribe, or a tribe named after a town, the exact location of which is not known. All we can say is that it already existed in the twentieth century B.C. Similarly, the name of Abraham's father (Terah) may have been derived from the town of *Til-Turahi*, that of Abraham's great-grandfather (Serug) from the town of *Sarugi* (West of Haran) and that of Peleg (Serug's grandfather) from the town of *Paliga* (mentioned by late geographers) at the confluence of the Khabur with the Euphrates.

Modern Biblical scholars view these Biblical events as connected with the large-scale migrations of the twentieth century B.C.[3] At or about that time, the Amorites were pouring into Babylonia, swallowing up important cities, Babylon included (*c.* 1700 B.C.). Syria and Palestine, too, received an influx of this people. Naturally, the migrants

[1] J. Hoftijzer: *Die Verheissungen und die drei Erzväter*, Leyden, 1956.

[2] J. C. L. Gibson: "Light from Mars on the Patriarchs"; *JSS*, VII, 1962, pp. 44–63.

[3] For Israel's position among her neighbours, cf. S. Moscati: *Geschichte und Kultur der Semitischen Völker*, Stuttgart, 1953.

adopted many of their hosts' customs, rites and beliefs, and much of their languages.

Much fresh light has been thrown on the history of the Patriarchs by archaeological texts discovered in Northern Mesopotamia. Clay tablets dating from the sixteenth and fifteenth century B.C. dug up in the ruins of *Nuzu* (not far from the modern Kirkuk) have shown that the laws of Nuzu were very similar to those implicit in stories about the Patriarchs.[1] From the Nuzu tablets we can see why the *teraphim* (household gods) played so important a role in the story of Jacob and Laban (Gen. 31 : 19, 30, 32, 34–35). According to Nuzu law, Laban, who had no son of his own, could adopt Jacob by marrying him to one of his daughters. If, however, a son was born to Laban subsequently, that son would share Jacob's inheritance and receive the *teraphim*. From Gen. 30–35, we may conclude that Laban did in fact beget a son or sons during the long time that Jacob stayed with him, and that Jacob's position was therefore endangered. When Jacob fled from Laban's house taking the *teraphim* with him, he showed his determination not to surrender what he considered his by right. Since the laws involved were taken for granted by the author of Gen. 29–31, he felt no need to mention them explicitly. Similarly, Hittite law helps to explain many of the Patriarchs' actions, e.g. why Ephron the Hittite presented to Abraham not only a cave but an entire field as a burying place for Sarah (Gen. 23 : 11). According to Hittite law, a property buyer invariably took over an obligation, though we do not know of what kind.

As we have seen, the Patriarchs were pastoral nomads. Whenever we watch modern Bedouins pulling up their stakes as they prepare to look for new grazing grounds, we are

[1] *ANET*, pp. 219–220.

forcibly reminded of the Biblical scene. The famous wall-paintings in the tomb at Beni Hassan in Egypt (*c.* 1890 B.C.) depicting the arrival of a Semitic family—men, women, children and small donkeys—at the Egyptian border could almost have been the work of a modern artist depicting the contemporary scene.[1] The report by the Egyptian, Sinuhe, who visited Syria at about the same time, also depicts the Israelites as nomads. While he despised their primitive way of life, he praised their hospitality.[2] A note of disdain was struck in a Mesopotamian song according to which the sons of the desert have their swords as comrades, know no discipline, eat raw meat, and neither live in houses nor bury their dead.

Though the Book of Genesis suggests that the Patriarchs paid frequent visits to Egypt (Gen. 12 : 10–20) and Mesopotamia, we are told that they spent most of their time in Palestine. Abraham lived near Mamre, south of Jerusalem (Gen. 13 : 18), Isaac near Beer-sheba (Gen. 26 : 23), and Jacob near Bethel and Shechem (Gen. 33 : 18; 35 : 1).[3] Countless altars, sacred stones and holy places in the mountains of Palestine give evidence of the life in Patriarchal times in these regions. It is extremely difficult, however, to say to what extent the local legends about these shrines do, in fact, go back to Israel's earliest history.

The Biblical account of Abraham contains but a single hint about events that impinge upon political history. According to Gen. 14, four Mesopotamian kings went out against Sodom and Gomorrah, the home of Lot, Abraham's nephew. They came from the East along the "King's highway"

---

[1] *ANEP*, Fig. 3.

[2] *ANET*, pp. 18–20. Cf. also the report of Wen Amon's visit to Phoenicia (*ANET*, pp. 25–28).

[3] A. Alt: "Der Gott der Väter," *KS*, I, pp. 1–78.

(which is also mentioned in Num. 20 : 17). The allied kings, who scored initial successes against the two towns, are mentioned by name: Chedorlaomer, King of Elam; Amraphel, King of Shinar; Arioch, King of Ellasar; and Tidal, King of Nations. It was previously thought that Amraphel of Shinar was identical with King Hammurabi of Babylon, but this idea has not had much support recently. The placing of Sodom and Gomorrah has proved as difficult as the identification of the four kings. It seems unlikely that the towns were buried beneath the southern tip of the Dead Sea. However, the terrain round *Sedum*—nowadays the site of a large potash works at the foot of a salt-mountain some 650 feet high and some 7 miles long—which has not altered appreciably in historical times, was admirably suited to give rise to popular legends of the kind reported in Gen. 19 : 23–25.

The connection between the Patriarchs and the founding of the Hebrew religion is emphasised in Exod. 3 : 6. For when God appeared to Moses in the burning bush, He identified Himself as "the God of thy father, the God of Abraham, the God of Isaac and the God of Jacob." From fairly recent Greek texts we know that the phrase "I am the God of . . ." was commonly used to indicate that an anonymous power had revealed itself to an individual, and through him to his tribe.

Moses identified this power with Yahweh, the God who had revealed himself to him, and his experience together with those of Abraham (Gen. 15, etc.) became the basis of Israel's religion.[1]

It would, however, be a mistake to conclude that the religious beliefs of the Patriarchs were totally distinct from those of the Canaanites. Archaeological investigations have shown clearly that there was a very close connection between

[1] Cf. A. Alt: "Der Gott der Väter," *KS*, I, pp. 1–78.

the rites of the Patriarchs and those of the rest of the population. Thus Genesis, even in its final form, contains passages mentioning many rites long since forgotten by the Jews. For instance, when Jacob woke up from his sleep in Bethel (Gen. 28 : 18) and again after his covenant with Laban (Gen. 31 : 44, ff.) he erected a stone pillar. Many similar stones marking the locality where a divine revelation was received by someone have been discovered all over Palestine. Moreover, the God of the Fathers was known not only as Yahweh but also as Shaddai and El Elyon. The name "El" was the title of the godhead of the Canaanites. The close connection between the religions of Israel and Canaan can still be detected in the Book of Genesis, written long after the events it describes, and this is precisely why we can look upon the Patriarchs as historical figures. True, the Bible contains a host of legendary associations with all sorts of phenomena and popular names, but out of its pages there rise up great historical figures—men who shone as leaders of their tribes and hence continued to live in the tradition.

The Patriarchal history culminates with the story of Joseph which revolves about the words he addressed to his brothers: "As for you, you meant evil against me; but God meant it for good, to bring it about that many people should be kept alive, as they are today" (Gen. 50 : 20). The Joseph story was undoubtedly given its current form by authors belonging to the wisdom-tradition, whose thoughts are also expressed in the Book of Proverbs. For Joseph, who withstood temptation, who was purged by visions, who remained temperate, and who sought to follow the secret paths of God, was the prototype of all men of wisdom.[1] Though the

[1] G. von Rad: "Josephsgeschichte und ältere Chokma," *VT, Supplementary Volume*, 1953, pp. 120–127.

Joseph story may also have been written under the influence of the Egyptian tale of the brothers Anubis and Bitis,[1] all attempts so far to find references to Joseph in Egyptian literature have been unsuccessful. All we know is that, for a time, Egypt was under the yoke of the Hyksos (who probably arrived there from Mesopotamia) and that the Egyptians preferred to pass over this period of foreign dominion in silence. There is no reason to doubt the Biblical story that during a time of great hunger, all, or at least some, of the tribes of Jacob or Israel were forced to take refuge in Egypt. Here they joined forces with an entirely different element called the "Hebrews"—a despised caste of casual labourers—in whose company they later fled from Egypt to join those members of the tribes who had remained in Palestine.

According to Gen. 29:14–30:24 and 35:16–20, the lineage of the twelve tribes was:

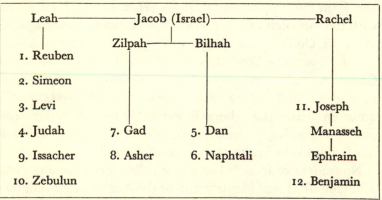

There is no reason to think that this family tree was made up by relatively late writers. Most probably it goes back to before Joshua.

[1] *ANET*, pp. 23–24.

III

MOSES THE LIBERATOR

THE life of Moses, like that of every religious founder, remains shrouded in mystery. Though in one opinion there can be no doubt about his historicity, we have few accurate chronological clues about his actual life.

Moses certainly lived at the time of the Israelite exodus from Egypt, which he is said to have brought about with Yahweh's help. This event became a central element of Israel's religion, as we can gather not only from the First Commandment but also from David's prayer (2 Sam. 7 : 23) and from the prophecies of Hosea (Hos. 11 : 1). Compared with the salvation of His people from Egyptian bondage, all other of God's great deeds pale into insignificance—the words "I am the Lord that brought thee out of Ur of the Chaldees . . ." (Gen. 15 : 7) are reminiscent of the beginning of the Ten Commandments. The Old Testament is quite emphatic that the religion of Israel, as a historical phenomenon, begins with the Exodus from Egypt, and that the Exodus is inconceivable without Moses.

No student of Israel's history can therefore ignore the two problems of Moses' identity and of the origins of his religious beliefs. Unfortunately these problems cannot be solved by asking Ranke's question how precisely it all happened, since, apart from the Bible, we have no independent and historically reliable reference to Moses. In fact, there are no non-

Biblical references even to the Exodus. Egyptian historiographers, who usually go into such great detail, keep complete silence about events which must have had serious repercussions on Egypt, if the Biblical account is correct. Indeed, the only Egyptian mention of Israel is an inscription on a stele commemorating Pharaoh Merneptah's victory over the Lybians in *c.* 1220 B.C. This inscription brackets Israel with Canaan, Gezer and Yenoam, but while Canaan, Gezer and Yenoam are described by a hieroglyph meaning "country," Israel is described by the symbol for "people."[1] Hence we may conclude that, by about 1220 B.C., Israel had become a nation. There is no certainty, however, whether the stele was erected before or after the Exodus from Egypt.

Nor do the historical difficulties due to the absence of extra-Biblical sources disappear entirely when we try to scan the books of Genesis and Exodus for references to the contemporary social scene. At best, we may say that Egyptian documents quite often describe Semitic immigrants in a way that bears out stories in Genesis. Thus a text written during the reign of Seti II (*c.* 1215 B.C.) might well have referred to Jacob's sons: "We have granted the passage of the Bedouin tribes from Edom through the fort of Merneptah in Zeku to the fenlands of the Per-Atum (Pithom) of Merneptah in Zeku . . . so that they may preserve their own lives and water their flocks." This report by an Egyptian frontier official to his superior, is an authentic eye-witness report of life on the Egyptian border.

---

[1] *ANET*, p. 378. However, J. A. Wilson has observed that the use of the hieroglyph for "people" instead of the hieroglyph for "country" may have been a mere spelling error. Merneptah's stele contains many such mistakes.

Again, the name "Hebrew" in Exodus is believed to be identical with Egyptian "pr" and the related Akkadian word *Habitu*,[1] both of which were sociological and not ethnological designations. The term is applied to persons or groups in Mesopotamia, in Palestine, and particularly in Egypt, and apparently meant "labourers," though not quite slaves. Assuming the identity of the Hebrews of the Bible with this element we still get no effective help for dating the events recorded in Exod. 1 : 8 ff, covering six centuries—the sixteenth to the eleventh.

The Old Testament, too, keeps strangely silent about the exact date of the Exodus. It fails to mention both the names of the Pharaoh whose dreams Joseph interpreted and also of the one from whose tyranny Moses saved his people. This is surprising because the Old Testament otherwise preserves numerous Egyptian names of persons, places and offices.[2] The only chronological clue that carries any weight is found in Exodus 1 : 11, which mentions the Pharaonic treasure cities of Pithom and Raamses. The latter city was founded by Pharaoh Rameses II (1290–1224 B.C.). From this reference many scholars have concluded that Rameses II must have been the Pharaoh who oppressed the Israelites.

More serious still than the lack of chronological data in the Bible is the absence of any Egyptian references to the catastrophic defeat of Pharaoh's army during his pursuit of

[1] See H. H. Rowley: *From Joseph to Joshua*, London, 1950 (Schweith Lectures), pp. 45–56.

[2] Joseph's wife was called Asenath (Gen. 41 : 45), i.e. property of the goddess Neit (Egyptian: ns-nt). Potiphar, Joseph's master, and Potipherah, Joseph's father-in-law, bore names made up of the type *pete* plus the name of a god—in this case Ra. Joseph's Egyptian name was Zaphnath-paaneah (Gen. 41 : 45), probably from the Egyptian *d(d)pnute-efanch* meaning "the god speaketh and he liveth."

the fleeing Hebrews. Since there is a wealth of Egyptian historical documents covering the period concerned, it seems most odd that so important an event should have been completely ignored. Nor can the silence of the Egyptian court historians be explained away by saying that no official histories ever record humiliating defeats. The events described in the Bible were much too far-reaching for any historian to have ignored them altogether. In these circumstances, some scholars have seen fit to deny the historicity of Moses completely, particularly such a leading historian of the Ancient World as Eduard Meyer (1906).[1] So extreme a point of view, however, does not appeal to most Biblical scholars. Far more confusing than such scepticism are the attempts to bridge the gaps between Biblical and non-Biblical sources with tenuous theories.[2] Only those syntheses which are in accordance with Biblical data are of any real value to the Biblical historian. An outstanding example of the correct approach is H. H. Rowley's thesis that Joseph rose to power in 1370 B.C. under Amenophis IV (Ikhnaton); that the Hebrews (Simeon and Levi), unable to hold Shechem, fled to Egypt in *c.* 1360 B.C.; that Moses was born in *c.* 1290 B.C., that the Exodus took place in *c.* 1230 B.C.; that the tribes were led into Canaan two years later by Joshua; and that Merneptah's victory, commemorated on his stele, came later.[3]

Central to most of these events, however, was the figure

---

[1] See his *Die Israeliten und ihre Nachbarstämme,* 1906.

[2] Noth, *GI,* pp. 100–102, has reconstructed his version of Exodus from Exod. 14 : 5 (the people fled); Exod. 14 : 9 (the Egyptians, without their Pharaoh, pursued after them); and Ex. 15 : 21 (the horse and its riders hath He thrown into the sea). But, by picking and choosing in the Old Testament, any kind of report can be pieced together.

[3] H. H. Rowley, *op. cit.,* p. 30 f.

of Moses.[1] The etymological origins of his name are uncertain. The story of his birth suggests that the name was
derived from the Hebrew verb *mshh*, meaning "to draw out
of," for in Ex. 2 : 10 we are told: ". . . And she called his
name *Mosheh*, and she said: Because I drew him out of the
water." In that case, however, his name ought to have
been *Mashui* ("drawn out") for Mosheh really means "he
who draws out." In this connection Martin Buber has
drawn attention to a strange reference to Moses in Isa.
63 : 12,[1] rendered in the A.V. "Then he remembered the
days of old, Moses *and* his people." The Hebrew has no
"and" and Buber thinks that in this passage Mosheh is not
the name but a title "the drawer forth of his people." Again,
Ps. 18 : 16 (= 2 Sam. 22 : 17) uses the verb *mshh* to describe the drawing of a person out of the waters (figuratively
speaking). There is no evidence to show that the name of
Moses was derived from the Egyptian word *ms* = son,
which was often affixed to names of such gods as Ptah, Ra
and Thot. Hence there is little basis for Freud's argument
that Moses was an Egyptian and a disciple of Ikhnaton.[2]

Though we do not think that the name of Moses was of
Egyptian origin, it would nevertheless pay us to scan the
many Egyptian names and words used in the Pentateuch
for any possible clues about the date of the exodus. In an
important paper, B. Stricker has shown that Egyptian words
underwent certain phonetic changes which can also be noted
in the Old Testament.[3] If we can take it that the Israelites
brought these terms to Palestine in the middle of the

[1] M. Buber: *Moses*, Zürich, 1948, pp. 50–52.
[2] The only passage which might seem to support Freud's thesis, viz.,
Ex. 2 : 19, is never mentioned by him.
[3] B. H. Stricker: "Trois études de phonetique et de morphologie
coptes," *Acta Orientalia*, XV, 1937, pp. 1 ff.

twelfth century B.C., the actual date of the exodus still remains a problem but we can at least infer the date of its recording.

It is generally believed that the gist of the story of the burning bush is part of the oldest and most genuine Mosaic tradition. For the rest, the Biblical authors have embellished the life of Moses with the kind of glitter that was expected to surround the biographies of most eastern kings and heroes. Thus, the story of the ark of bulrushes in which Moses was hidden in the water has a close parallel in the infancy story of King Sargon I of Akkad, who reigned over Babylonia in the twenty-fourth century B.C.[1] The ark, daubed with mud and pitch, may have been a round *guffa* of the kind used on the rivers and canals of Iraq to this day. The story of the burning bush on Mt. Horeb, on the other hand, is unique in eastern literature. Perhaps the only reference to Mt. Sinai in Exod. 3 is indirect—the Hebrew term for bush is *seneh*. It was at this holy mountain which is known by many names —including Sinai, Horeb and Seir—and which has never been placed convincingly, that Moses fused a number of pre-Mosaic traditions into a new religion.

In the Biblical account of the events on Mt. Horeb we must clearly distinguish between essential and incidental elements. All descriptions of the divine presence are invariably embellished with details that have no bearing on the revelation itself. For this reason alone, we need not dwell particularly on the role of fire in the theophany narratives. Stade and Eerdmans were wrong in stressing the importance of the pillars of smoke and fire enveloping Sinai and causing it to burn like a furnace (Exod. 19 : 18), and Eerdmans, in particular, was wrong to conclude from the Biblical reference

[1] *ANET*, p. 119.

to the forges of the Kenites that Moses was influenced by Kenite religious conceptions.[1] In so doing he went beyond the known facts, for all we really know of the Kenites is that they were allies of the Israelites (cf. Judges 5 : 24 and 1 Sam. 15 : 6). True, the many references to Moses' father-in-law—called Jethro, Jether, Reuel and Hobab—may well have been introduced to emphasise the special position of the Kenites among the people of Israel, but all attempts to relate Moses' religious beliefs to those of the Kenites are tantamount to substituting one unknown quantity for another—a singularly unrewarding method.

E. Auerbach, the author of an important book on Moses,[2] holds that the only Biblical evidence of Moses' historical existence is a reference to his Levitic origins (Exod. 2 : 1), the textually doubtful, and historically much later, reference to a grandson of Manasseh (Moses?) in Judges 18 : 30, may slightly broaden this narrow base. Auerbach's argument is roughly this: in pre-Mosaic times, the Levites, who formed a closed tribe, lived in the oasis of Kadesh, whence they were driven out by the Amalekites. Members of the tribe then migrated to central Arabia, Palestine and Egypt, but preserved their old ways. It was these traditions which Moses drew upon, for, according to the Bible, both his parents were of the house of Levi.

On this assumption, it seems reasonable to conclude that the final objective of the exiles from Egypt was not Palestine but the oasis of Kadesh. In Exod. 5 : 3 we can read that the Israelites pleaded with the Pharaoh to grant them three days' journey into the desert. This request may admittedly

[1] B. D. Eerdmans: *Alttestamentliche Studien*, II, *Die Vorgeschichte Israels*, 1908; id., III, *Das Buch Exodus*, 1910.
[2] E. Auerbach: *Moses*, Amsterdam, 1953.

have been a deliberate attempt to hide their true destination, but, in fact, the Bible goes on to describe a long sojourn in Kadesh-barnea. The Israelites remained there for some forty years before they dared to make the final attempt to reach Palestine. According to Auerbach, the story of the Israelites' long and devious journey merely reflects the Biblical author's wish to spin out his heroic tale. The following items are fitted into this reconstruction: the Israelites' hatred of the Amalekites, which is held to have arisen from pre-Mosaic attacks on Kadesh; the mention of Levites in Minaean inscriptions, apparently as priests; the fact that the Levites held a special position among the tribes of Israel, since all the other tribes lived in their own tribal territories, while they were scattered among the tribes. Unlike Stade and Eerdmans, according to whom the religion of Israel developed from that of the Kenites, Auerbach argues that the Mosaic faith was based on Levite traditions. He finds much similarity between the origins of Judaism and of Mohammedanism. In Mohammedanism too, a religious movement culminated in the creation of a nation. Kadesh may be compared to Mecca, and the Levites to the tribe of Kuraish who guarded the holy places. Both Mohammed and Moses began as reformers within their own tribes, and finally became rulers, legislators, generals and prophets of the nation at large. From Mohammed's life, which is within the grasp of modern historical research, we may make a number of other valuable inferences about Moses, whose biography is far more elusive. It seems unlikely that fresh evidence about Moses will be discovered in the near future. The famous Sinaitic inscriptions of the Hyksos Age are bound to prove disappointing in this respect, even when they have been satisfactorily deciphered.

So far, all historical reconstructions of the exodus—
including Auerbach's—have been biased by the particular
views of their authors. There is no shred of evidence that
Moses was in any way related to the Levites of Kadesh and,
in any case, once we agree with Auerbach that the eulogies
written by later generations on which we base our account of
Moses' motives and actions are historically doubtful we
might as well scrap Auerbach's whole explanation. At most,
we can agree with him that the dispersion of the Levites was
incorporated into Biblical history.

Much of our ignorance of Moses' true life is due to the fact
that the Biblical story has been highly coloured by the
veneration of later generations. It is significant that the
Bible mentions neither Aaron's nor Moses' grave. Aaron
died, we are told, on Mt. Hor (Num. 20:22–28), and
Moses died on Mt. Nebo, "and the Lord buried him"
(Deut. 34:6). (Subsequent legends have embellished the
Biblical account—cf. Jude 9 and the pseudepigraphic
Assumption of Moses.) From this omission, Goethe concluded
that Moses must have committed suicide, and Sellin and
Freud that he was murdered by his own people. The Bible
explains that "his eye was not dim nor his natural force
abated" when he died at the age of 120 years (Deut. 34:7).
All we can, in fact, gather from the Bible is that Moses was
often opposed by his people (Num. 20:1–12) and even by
Aaron and Miriam who objected to his marrying an
Ethiopian woman (Num. 12). Quite generally, we may say
that Aaron's attitude towards Moses is never quite fully
explained in the Bible, and therefore poses special problems.
While Exod. 32:19 portrays Moses as prone to anger,
Num. 12:3 describes him as very meek.

The giving of the law, recorded in the books of Exodus,

Leviticus, Numbers and Deuteronomy, is attributed to Moses by all the Biblical writers. This law is said to have been based on God's covenant with the people of Israel on Mt. Sinai fifty days after the exodus from Egypt, an event commemorated by the synagogue during the Feast of Weeks. The actual wording of the law, which was engraved on two stone tablets kept in the Holy of Holies until the Babylonians destroyed the Temple in 587 B.C., remains unknown. Not even the size of the tablets or the nature of the script is recorded anywhere. According to Exod. 32 : 15, the tables were "written on both sides"—which would seem to indicate that they contained more than the Ten Commandments, but according to Deut. 10 : 4 the Lord Himself wrote only the Ten Commandments upon them. The Book of Deuteronomy, however, seemingly refers to other tablets—"the tables of the covenant"—which must have contained a larger number of laws (Deut. 9 : 9).

Until the actual tablets are unearthed—which, after all, is a possibility—every theory about the original law must remain highly speculative. All our attempts to reconstruct the basic law by other criteria turn the Mosaic problem into a jigsaw-puzzle. In order to piece it together as best we can from Biblical data, we must clearly distinguish new from old, and original legislation from its later embellishments. Above all, we must distinguish between the specifically Israelitic elements and those received from neighbouring peoples. This method of research has been applied successfully to a great deal of material dug up in countries surrounding ancient Israel. Albrecht Alt has drawn attention to the "apodictic" character of the specifically Israelitic laws, but this is no proof that the apodictic formulae in the Ten Commandments and in other laws of the Pentateuch go back to the time of Moses.[1] Martin David has stressed the difference between the social background of the laws of Israel and that of the laws of Hammurabi—showing the Mosaic code as a characteristic peasant code.[2] Now, it is generally held that it was near Sinai and Transjordan that the transformation from nomadic into agricultural life first began. Auerbach has argued that Israel's earliest legislation incorporated nomadic ideals. According to him, the tenth commandment was originally no more than: Thou shalt not covet a house! In that way, it does, in fact, conform to the terse form of the preceding commandments, but this kind of interpretation is surely far too radical to have any great merit.

All in all, it is difficult to determine which laws are the oldest—all we can say is that Israel's laws and those of her neighbours are based on common religious and moral norms. For that very reason we cannot speak of copying. Laws are endowed with meaning from within—civilisations may be compared with closed, though sometimes overlapping, circles. Hence while the laws of different civilisations may be identical in letter, they invariably differ in spirit. Now the spirit of Israel's law was love of Yahweh, who led his people out of Egypt. Worship of Yahweh was exclusive—no other Gods were allowed to exist before Him. Yahweh's unquestioned authority was such that He could enforce submission to His moral laws which, moreover, were so universally valid, that they could become the basis of Christian civilisation.

In the history of Israel, Moses is first and foremost the great legislator and the agent of God. It is he who, by

[1] A. Alt: *Die Ursprünge des israelitischen Rechts, KS*, I, pp. 278–332.

forging a bond between God and His people, managed to fuse the Egyptian exiles into one nation. The covenant was made on Mt. Horeb or Mt. Sinai, a holy mountain which was much later said to have been on the Sinai peninsula. The covenant was based on the original religious experiences of those Patriarchs whom the people of Israel called their fathers. All the subsequent history of Israel—the journeys through strange regions, the stay in the desert, and finally the settling in Palestine—can only be understood in terms of its bond with God. Even the most critical evaluation of the data cannot shake our faith in this unique fact. Through the covenant Israel was transformed into a nation.

IV

THE CONQUEST OF THE HOLY LAND

BIBLICAL reports about Israel's sojourn in the desert suggest that the first attempt to enter Canaan was thwarted: "Then the Amalekites and the Canaanites who dwelt in that hill country came down and smote them, and defeated them even and pursued them, unto Hormah" (Num. 14:45). The failure is attributed to internal disputes.

Of the twelve spies, only Joshua and Caleb had advised an attack; the other ten had spoken of Canaan as "land that devours its inhabitants" (Num. 13:32). The country was said to be inhabited by giants (the sons of Anak or Anahim) and hence beyond the reach of the poorly armed invaders. The demoralisation following their defeat probably forced the tribes to stay on in the desert. Only much later did they make a second attempt to conquer the promised land, and this time they were successful.

We cannot help being struck by the differences between the Israelites' advance into Palestine and the usual raids of nomads driven on by hunger or a thirst for loot. Israel's campaigns were no plundering raids but attempts to find a permanent home and permanent pastures. This difference is due to two causes: the traditional belief of the tribes that Canaan was the home of their forefathers, and the (generally neglected) desire to join up with related tribes in the country, which has not yet been fully explained by critical writers.

The unsystematic and often revised data in the Pentateuch, the Book of Joshua, or Judges[1] do not lend themselves to a satisfactory reconstruction of the actual events. However, the Biblical data are in general agreement with archaeological findings. We know today that Palestine, in the fourteenth and thirteenth century B.C., was made up of a large number of small city states inhabited by Canaanites, and governed by princes and courtiers like so many mediaeval fiefs. The princes owed allegiance to Egypt, and the Pharaohs would deal with them leniently or harshly, as the occasion demanded.

Our most important historical sources for the fourteenth century B.C. are the Armarna letters[2] consisting of some 350 documents dating back to the reigns of the Pharaohs Amenophis III (1413–1377) and Amenophis IV (Ikhnaton, 1377–1360). The letters, clay tablets inscribed with cuneiform characters, were written in official Akkadian, except for diplomatic messages from Palestine, which contained many Canaanite terms. Jerusalem was called *Urusalimu*, and there were references to the *Apiru*—or Hebrews—a term used here to describe tribes without tribal lands and hence a nuisance to the government. The overall impression produced by the Armarna Letters is that the many city states of Palestine were frequently at war with one another, so that the entire country was in near-chaos. We also learn that, since important trade routes met in Palestine, more strangers came there than to any other country of the ancient East. Palestine's powerful neighbours established

---

[1] Cf. A. Alt: "Die Landnahme der Israeliten in Palästina," *KS*, I, pp. 89–126, and "Erwägungen über die Landnahme der Israeliten in Palästina," *KS*, I, pp. 126–175.

[2] J. A. Knudtzon: *Die El-Armarna Tafeln*, 2 vols. Leipzig, 1915.

colonies, headed by merchants who represented their country's interests. Among the most powerful of these traders were the Egyptians.

The cities were generally small, though fortified by imposing walls. The impression they made on the advancing Israelites is described in Deut. 1 : 28 and in Num. 13 : 28. Since the roaming Israelites lacked weapons for meeting the Canaanites in open battle, they preferred to wage guerilla warfare in the mountains. Thus we are told in Judges 1 : 19 that the Israelites could not drive out the inhabitants of the valley "because they had chariots of iron." Even much later—in the ninth century B.C.—it was still said in Syria that the gods of the Israelites are gods of the hills who can only be defeated on the plain (1 Kings 20 : 23).

The Israelites were led into Canaan by Joshua, the son of Nun, Moses' servant. Though the Bible tells us little about the man himself, it gives us a full account of his strategy. Apparently the Israelites advanced from three directions; from the south, from Transjordan in the east, and finally from the north.

Joshua 6 describes the events in the eastern sector where Jericho and Ai are said to have fallen into Israelite hands. From excavations in these two towns, we know that Ai was inhabited from 3300 until 2400 B.C., and not again until the Israelites settled there in 1000 B.C. The problem of fitting these findings into Joshua 8 has been discussed by Alt, who held that the use of the phrase "unto this day" (Joshua 8 : 29) stamps the Biblical account as a legend recorded in later times,[1] and by W. F. Albright[2] whose suggestion that

[1] A. Alt: Joshua, *KS*, I, pp. 176–192.
[2] W. F. Albright: "The Israelite Conquest of Canaan in the Light of Archaeology," *BASOR*, 74, 1939, pp. 11 ff.

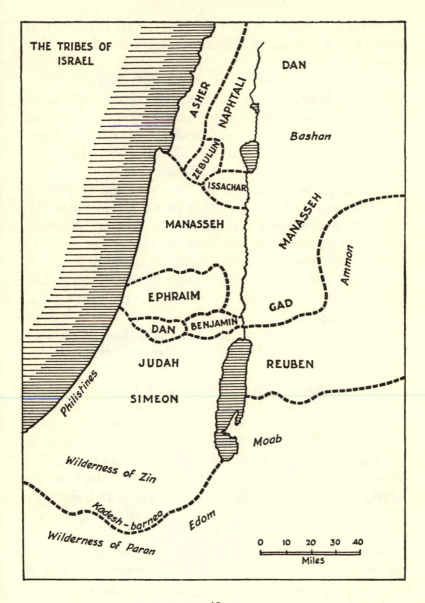

THE TRIBES OF ISRAEL

DAN

ASHER

NAPHTALI

Bashan

ZEBULUN

ISSACHAR

MANASSEH

MANASSEH

Ammon

EPHRAIM

GAD

DAN BENJAMIN

JUDAH

REUBEN

SIMEON

Philistines

Moab

Wilderness of Zin

Kadesh-barnea

Edom

Wilderness of Paran

0   10   20   30   40
Miles

Ai was in fact Bethel is founded on the slender evidence that Bethel was destroyed by attackers in the thirteenth century B.C.

The problem of Jericho is more difficult still. When Garstang resumed Sellin's excavations at the ruins of Tell es-Sultân (just outside the Arab village of Rihā and not far from the Jericho of Herod the Great) he thought that the archaeological evidence confirmed the Biblical story. However, subsequent excavations by Katherine M. Kenyon[1] have altered the picture radically. We know now that the ruins of Tell es-Sultân represent the oldest known city in the world, with a history that goes back possibly to 9000 B.C. A careful analysis of pottery fragments provided no evidence at all in favour of the historicity of the events described in Joshua 6. None of the earthenware dates back to the fifteenth, thirteenth or the second half of the fourteenth century B.C. This does not mean, of course, that Joshua 6 is a mere fabrication. However, no one can claim that archaeology has enabled him to date the capture of Jericho by the Israelites.

From the Book of Numbers, we learn that the Israelites tried to enter Canaan by the "King's highway" in southern Transjordan and that they were opposed by such local Kings as Sihon and Og (Num. 21 : 21–35). Opposition to the Israelite advance is also the background to the story of Balaam. Balaam had the magic gift of words which he was willing to sell to King Balak of Moab. Though his story is a legend rather than historical fact, it nevertheless gives us a picture of contemporary conditions.

Of far greater historical worth are Chapters 10 and 11 of the Book of Joshua which describes the southern advance of

[1] M. Kenyon: *Digging up Jericho*, London, 1957.

the Israelites. We are told that, when Gibeon made peace with Israel, the Amorite kings of Jerusalem, Hebron, Jarmuth, Lachish and Eglon, who felt threatened by the alliance, made war on Gibeon. They were defeated by the Israelites near Makkedah, which has not yet been identified with certainty. Then the Israelites conquered Libnah in the Valley of the Terebinth (the scene of David's struggle with Goliath); the city of Lachish (the ruins of which were dug up in Tell ed-Duweir, half-way between Jerusalem and Gaza); the city of Eglon (the modern Tell el Hesi); the city of Hebron and the city of Debir or Kiriath-sepher (possibly the modern Tell Beit Mirsim). Archaeological investigations of the ruins of these towns seem to indicate that they were laid waste between 1250 and 1200 B.C., and were later rebuilt by another people. Since, however, the so-called Sea Peoples came down the Palestinian coast during the thirteenth century B.C., we cannot say with any certainty whether or not it was the Israelites who were responsible for the destruction of these towns. Lachish in particular poses special problems, for not only was an Egyptian temple found there (which was destroyed about 1200 B.C.) but also a jug with an Egyptian inscription, dated in Year 4 of the reign of a Pharaoh whose name is illegible, but who may well have been Merneptah (1224-1216 B.C.).

From the Biblical story, it appears that Joshua began his entry into Palestine by occupying the south. Later he marched north, though his exact route is unknown. All we know is that he laid siege to Hazor in the far north (Joshua 11). Its ruins were sought by Garstang in the gigantic Tell-el-Qedah, north of Lake Galilee and not far from Lake Huleh on the great caravan route leading to Syria, Asia Minor and Mesopotamia. The tremendous area of the

Tell el-Qedah ruins bears out the claim in Joshua 11 : 10 that "Hazor formerly was the head of all those kingdoms."[1] Recent excavations at Hazor, carried out by Israeli archaeologists under Yigael Yadin since 1955, have shown that the town was destroyed in the thirteenth century B.C., i.e. towards the end of the Bronze Age. Hence, if Joshua's campaign took place as early as that, the Biblical report would be fully supported by archaeological findings.

However, the Bible itself does not entitle us to select that date. For instance, 1 Kings 6 : 1 says: "And it came to pass in the four hundred and eightieth year after the children of Israel were come out of the land of Egypt, in the fourth year of Solomon's reign over Israel . . . that he began to build the house of the Lord." Since King Solomon began to build his Temple *c.* 959 B.C., according to our chronology it would appear that the Israelites left Egypt as early as 1439 B.C. However, the figure of 480 years representing twelve periods of forty years each, was probably chosen for symbolical rather than historical reasons. Even so, I cannot agree with those scholars who have arbitrarily substituted twelve generations of twenty-five years each, thus "proving" that the Biblical text agrees with archaeological discoveries.

Joshua failed to conquer all Palestine, and Joshua 13 : 1-7, and Judges 1 : 27-36 admit this quite openly. One of the towns surprisingly left to the Canaanites was Shechem, to which the Bible attaches great traditional importance (Joshua 24), since it was here that Joshua assembled the

[1] Cf. the significant report in Joshua 11 : 9 that "Joshua hamstrung their horses and burned their chariots with fire." This shows that the advancing nomads, who were used to asses, had no interest in the captured horses.

people to renew their covenant with God. As there is no reason to doubt the historical truth of this report, it would appear that the Shechemites were people akin to the advancing Israelites, and hence their allies.

Much of the book of Joshua describes the various regions allocated to the different tribes. From these accounts we can learn a great deal about the natural resources of Palestine, and, in particular, we hear that the Israelites cleared the forests and opened up new agricultural land (Joshua 17 : 15). Alt has argued convincingly that the list of tribal frontiers in Joshua 13–19 is based on older sources.[1] One Biblical report, in particular, is very suggestive: "The land of Tappuah belonged to Manasseh, but the town of Tappuah on the boundary of Manasseh belonged to the sons of Ephraim" (Joshua 17 : 8). From this, it would appear that the entire tribe of Manasseh must have seized the fields belonging to the city state of Tappuah. The original inhabitants had to withdraw to the town itself, which henceforth was cut off from its food supplies and thus fell an easy prey to the Ephraimites. As a result, the borders between Manasseh and Ephraim cut across a formerly united region—a phenomenon which struck the writer of Joshua 17 as deserving special mention. The list of towns in Joshua 15–21 ff. is generally held to represent the various administrative areas of the kingdom of Judah, in accordance with, or adapted to, earlier traditions.

With the allocation of the whole of Palestine west of the Jordan to those tribes which had taken part in the conquest of the country, the first phase of the occupation was completed. But though the whole country was parcelled out to

[1] A. Alt: "Das System der Stammesgrenzen im Buche Josua," *KS*, I, pp. 193–202.

the newcomers in theory, the Canaanites managed to hold on to the most important towns and to keep control of the trade routes in practice. Moreover, the Israelites had failed to occupy the fertile coastal plain—their settlements remained on the slopes of the mountains.

V

THE TIME OF THE JUDGES

BEFORE Israel became a kingdom, it was governed by "Judges." They were generally military leaders, whose authority was based, not on hereditary titles, but on a special call by God. By and large, their power was restricted to small parts of Palestine, even though later editors have given the impression that they ruled over the whole country.

All our reconstructions of this complex period, when Israel lacked a central government, are based on the Book of Judges. That book, however, is the result of radical revisions by men who were anxious to fit the facts to their standard religious theme: Israel's betrayal of Yahweh—Yahweh's wrath and punishment—Israel's return to Yahweh—Yahweh's reconciliation with Israel through His judge. This scheme was applied to a period of history which, according to the book, lasted for 420 years, but which, in fact, must have been very much shorter.

Apart from mentioning the deeds of the various judges, the Book of Judges also refers to traditional legends associated with a number of holy places. Thus the palm tree between Bethel and Ramah, to which pilgrims came to pay homage, was connected with the name of Deborah. The Deborah originally meant was Rebekah's nurse (cf. Gen. 35: 8). But in Judges 4: 4–5 we are told that the prophetess Deborah "judged" under that tree, which thus was imagined to have been named after her. However, the home of the prophetess was much farther to the north. Again, the holy oak in Ophra, belonging to Joash the Abiezrite (Judges 6: 11), is said to have played an important role in the story of Gideon. It was beneath it that Gideon was summoned to take up arms against the Midianites, and that he later set up his *ephod* (Judges 8 : 27). Abimelech was made king by the "oak of the pillar at Shechem" (Judges 9 : 6). The Samson stories mention the burying place of Manoah, between Zorah and Eshtaol and a nearby sacred rock (Judges 16: 31; 13: 19), as well as the miraculous spring called En-hakkore "which is at Lehi to this day" (Judges 15: 19). The book also describes the setting up of idols in Dan (Chapters 17–18) and mentions a strange local custom: the annual departure of the daughters of Israel for the mountains to bewail the fate of Jephthah's daughter who had died a virgin (Judges 11: 37–40). From such passages as Judges 21: 12 and 21 describing the dancing and abduction of virgins in the region of Shiloh, we may well conclude that some Israelite groups practised Canaanite fertility rites. The Book of Judges, therefore, gives us descriptions not only of battles, but also of the customs and holy places of Israel in this time.

According to Judges 20: 27, the ark of the covenant was kept at Bethel. This symbol, which had travelled with the wandering tribes of Israel into Palestine, reappears at the beginning of the story of Samuel, the last and greatest of all the judges. Auerbach has argued that the Book of Judges was substituted for a lost book which dealt exclusively with the fate of the ark during its journey from Gilgal to Shiloh. According to him, this contention is borne out by an obscure passage, viz. Judges 2: 1–5: "And an angel of the Lord came up from Gilgal to Bochim . . ." (Bochim was a sacred place not far from Bethel.)

We do not know who collated the traditional stories about the judges and the holy places associated with them, but since the author of the Book of Judges was particularly interested in the temple in Shiloh (Judges 18: 31), he is likely to have been a priest.[1]

If we ignore changes and additions in Judges 1 that were intended to fit the text to later conditions, we can reconstruct the following picture of the conquest:

The Calebites and Kenites, and possibly also the tribes of Judah and Simeon, entered Palestine from the "city of Palms" in the south (Judges 1: 16). This city could not have been Jericho but must have been Tamar in the Negeb. The remaining tribes advanced from the east through Jericho. This picture must be pieced together by reading between the lines, since according to the later authors of the book of Joshua, all the tribes passed through Jericho.

After a brief mention of the defeat of Chushan-rishathaim, an otherwise unknown king of Mesopotamia, at the hands of Othniel, one of Israel's judges (Judges 3: 5–11) the Book of Judges goes on to describe the Benjaminite Ehud's uprising against Eglon, King of Moab. The Moabites had attacked the region west of the River Jordan and had captured the City of Palms—in this case evidently Jericho. All the surrounding tribes—including the Israelites—were forced to pay tribute to the hated usurper. On one occasion they sent Ehud, who was a left-handed man, to deliver the tribute to Eglon. He was granted a private audience by the King because he had a message of God for him. As the King rose up to listen to the

[1] Cf. E. Täubler: *Biblische Studien. Die Epoche der Richter*, Tübingen, 1958, p. lxv.

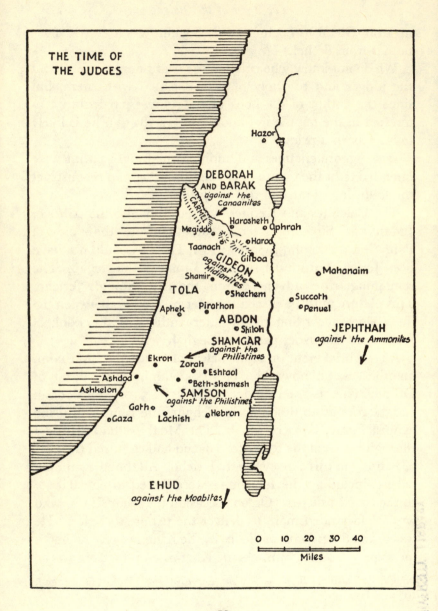

THE TIME OF
THE JUDGES

Hazor

DEBORAH
AND BARAK
*against the
Canaanites*

CARMEL

Harosheth   Ophrah
Megiddo
Harod
Taanach   Gilboa
GIDEON
against the
Midianites
Shamir   Mahanaim
TOLA   Shechem   Succoth
Aphek   Pirathon   Penuel
ABDON
Shiloh   JEPHTHAH
SHAMGAR   *against the Ammonites*
against the
Philistines
Ekron
Zorah
Ashdod   Eshtaol
Ashkelon   Beth-shemesh
SAMSON
against the Philistines
Gath   Lachish   Hebron
Gaza

EHUD
against the Moabites

0   10 20 30 40

Miles

52

will of God, Ehud stabbed him with a dagger he had con-
cealed on his right side. He was even able to make good his
escape. This murder was the signal for an attack on the
Moabites, who were driven out from their stronghold west of
the Jordan. Another reported victory was that of Shamgar

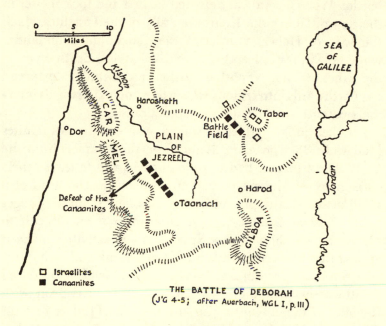

THE BATTLE OF DEBORAH
(J'G 4-5; after Auerbach, WGL I, p. III)

who "killed six hundred Philistines with an ox-goad"
(Judges 3: 31).

The prophetess Deborah is praised in Judges 4 and 5, first
in prose and then in a hymn of victory. Both accounts are
generally believed to have been composed during her life,
though differences between the two versions suggest that the
prose report is historically more reliable. The leader of the
Israelites at the time was Barak of the tribe of Naphtali, and
their greatest enemy was Sisera, captain of the host of King

53

Jabin of Hazor, who oppressed the Israelites for twenty years. It was against this king that Deborah declared a holy war, and ordered several tribes of Israel to capture the strategic Mt. Tabor in Galilee. Sisera replied by mounting an attack near the Kishon river, throwing all his iron chariots into the battle. When Sisera was defeated he fled and took shelter in the tent of Heber the Kenite, an ally of the Israelites. Jael, the wife of Heber, murdered the Canaanite commander while he was fast asleep.[1] Sisera's defeat and death enabled the tribes of Dan, Naphthali, Asher and Zebulun to spread out northwards into regions where they soon afterwards intermarried with the Canaanite population.

Another judge, Gideon, waged war on the Midianites (Judges 6: 8), who had advanced on their camels from the East. The Israelites had to hide in caves and to thresh their corn in secret (Judges 6: 2, 11). Gideon, at the head of a small army, finally put an end to this new scourge (Judges 7–8). (Gideon's home was in Ophrah, a town difficult to place, though Biblical descriptions of his activities make it appear that he lived farther south than Barak and Deborah.) As a result of their defeat, the Midianites never again dared to attack the people of Israel, who rewarded Gideon with the offer of the crown to him and his heirs (Judges 8: 22).[2] Gideon is said to have refused this offer, on the grounds that the Lord alone was the ruler over Israel. However, since one of his sons was called Abimelech (my father is king) it has been suggested that Gideon did, in fact, accept the crown.

[1] On the conflict between nomadic hospitality and the total demands of Yahwism, see S. Nyström: *Beduinentum und Jahwismus*, Lund, 1946. The author uses the story of Jael and Sisera as a paradigm not only of the conflict between nomadic and peasant law, but above all of the role of exclusive Yahweh worship.

[2] Cf. Martin Buber: *Königtum Gottes*, Zürich, 1956.

One of Gideon's wives was a non-Israelite, whose people helped her son Abimelech to hold on to his crown, after he had killed all his brothers except Jotham, who managed to escape. Abimelech's reign was cut short after only three years. His end was as bloody as its beginning: during his siege of Thebez, a woman threw down a millstone from the city's tower and smashed his skull.

The fratricidal struggle set off by Abimelech's accession to the throne had so weakened Israel that the Philistines had an easy victory over them at the battle of Aphek. As a result, the Philistines were able to advance deep into Palestine from their coastal strongholds. Before this time, however, Israel was governed by a number of less well-known judges, including Tola (Judges 10: 1–2); Jair who had "thirty sons that rode on thirty asses and they had thirty cities" (Judges 10: 3–5); Ibzan of Bethlehem who had "thirty sons and thirty daughters" (Judges 12: 8–10); Elon the Zebulonite (Judges 12: 11–12); and finally Abdon who had "forty sons and thirty grandsons, who rode on seventy asses" (Judges 12: 13–15). The Bible tells us nothing else about these men but concentrates instead on stories of Jephthah and Samson.

Jephthah, "a mighty warrior, but the son of a harlot," was cast out by his half-brothers because of his illegitimacy (Judges 11: 2). He then became a bandit leader. He was a kind of self-appointed police chief who adhered strictly to his own code of honour, and who ensured the safety of compliant peasants in return. He was finally called in to help in the struggle against the Ammonites, who were oppressing Israel in Transjordan, and managed to free his kinsmen. The story of Jephthah is memorable for the oath he swore, which led tragically to the sacrifice of his daughter (Judges 11: 30–40), and for the way in which the Ephraimites were caught at the Jordan ford by being made to pronounce the word "shibboleth" (Judges 12: 1–7).

Though he was judge for only a short time, the Bible deals at length with Samson, whose name was derived from the word *shemesh* (sun). Since Samson was a native of Beth-shemesh, the "house of the sun," so named after its solar temple, some scholars have argued that the story of Samson is one of many solar myths. Thus the accounts of Samson's birth (Judges 13: 1–25) and of his end (Judges 16: 23–31) are said to be typical of such legends. Even so, we would be wrong to conclude that Samson himself was a completely legendary character.[1]

According to the Bible, all Samson's battles were fought between the mountainous country of south-western Judea and the coastal plain, now crossed by the railway line from Jerusalem to Tel-Aviv. It was in the coastal plain that the Philistines who, according to tradition came from Caphtor (Amos 9: 7), had settled. Despite some recent objections, there is no doubt that Caphtor is to be identified with Crete. Perhaps the Philistines came there and left again or were driven out during the great thirteenth-century migrations.[2] When the Egyptians barred their way into Africa they settled in Gaza, Ashdod, Ashkelon, Gath and Ekron on the southern coastal plain of Palestine. According to Egyptian sources, this must have happened during the reign of Rameses III (1198–1167 B.C.). The Philistines were governed by *seranim*, a word held identical with Greek *tyrannoi* = "tyrants." In Samson's time, the relations between the Philistines and the

[1] In an article in the *Archiv für Orientforschung* (1944), pp. 324 ff., F. Dornseiff renews the idea that the story of Samson was based on that of Heracles.

[2] Cf. G. A. Wainwright in *Journal of Hellenic Studies*, 51, 1931, pp. 1 ff.; and A. Furumark: *Opuscula Archaeologica*, VI (No. 18), pp. 223 ff.

Israelites were still rather uncertain. While there were many contacts and even a number of mixed marriages, there were also constant fights, or rather village squabbles. During such disputes, particularly valiant men would often rise to the fore, of whom two of the best known are Samson, of the tribe of Dan, and Goliath.

When the Danites were later forced to migrate to the north of Palestine, evidently because of Philistine pressures, the Philistines advanced even farther into the interior of the country, driving a wedge between the northern and southern tribes of Israel. In Samson's day (*c.* 1180 B.C.), however, the Philistines were still concentrated in the coastal strip.

In the long run, the Philistines presented a far greater threat to Israel than the Samson legend suggests. For one thing they controlled all the iron supplies at a time when iron was of paramount importance—the Philistines arrived in Palestine at the beginning of the Iron Age. Also, as renowned metal craftsmen, they could charge extortionate sums for their products (1 Sam. 13: 19) and hence hold the rest of the country to ransom.

Then again, the Philistines managed to advance farther and farther towards the north so that, in the end, they controlled the entire coast as far as Mt. Carmel, and hence were masters of the great caravan route joining Mesopotamia to Egypt via Damascus. Later, when Abimelech's excesses weakened Israel, the Philistines marched right into the centre of the country.

It would seem that the time of the Judges was one of the stormiest in the history of Israel. The turmoil and the resulting social and political conditions are recorded at length in the Book of Judges, from which we can piece together the following picture:

The various related tribes were divided into families (*mishpahoth*), and these, in turn, were divided into *beth aboth* (patriarchal houses). As individual tribes settled in given regions, they set up geographical boundaries. Every tribe must have had its own leader, whose role was important only in wartime. For the rest, each did what seemed good in his own eyes. At the head of every family was an elder, who may be compared to a modern Sheik. Those who were not born within the tribe were treated as strangers with fixed rights (*ger*), as strangers without rights (*nokri*), or as slaves. Within the tribe, blood feuds and family obligations (cf. the story of Ruth), ensured the continuance of the family and the punishment of those who threatened its safety.

In the course of time, the bond between the various tribes became closer and deeper, and two larger units were forged—one in the south and one in the north. Later still, the first kings welded both units into what, for the time, was a large and mighty empire. The collapse of this empire after the death of Solomon was due partly to the survival of conflicts from the reign of King Saul.

The bond between the northern and southern tribes was rooted in their common memory of the exodus from Egypt, in their common worship of Yahweh, and possibly in their common care of the Holy Ark of the Covenant. For this reason, Alt and Noth have made much of the resemblance between the tribes of Israel and the Greek "amphictyony," a confederation of neighbouring tribes, who took turns in looking after a shrine, each serving for one or two months. Israel's division into twelve tribes, corresponding to the twelve months of the year, would then have reflected the sharing out of duties at the Ark of the Covenant in Gilgad and later in

Shiloh. Genesis abounds with lists of twelve tribes: the twelve tribes of Aram (Gen. 22: 20–24), of Ishmael (Gen. 25: 13–16), and Edom (Gen. 36: 10–14). Possibly the bond between the tribes of Israel developed out of "holy wars," which demanded a strong political and military alliance under one leader.

The shrines of the amphictyony were also places of pilgrimage, where the devout participated in common worship and sacrifice (cf. I Sam. 1). In Israel, the shrines were probably used for proclaiming the divine laws, adherence to which, more than anything else, distinguished the tribes of Israel from the other inhabitants of Palestine. The law, hallowed by the authority of Moses, was extraordinarily exclusive and uncompromising, and emphasised the gulf separating the Israelites from their neighbours.

What is far more amazing is that, soon after their arrival in Palestine, the Israelites became so exceptionally literate a people. From the mention in Judges 8: 14 of a young captive who had no difficulty in writing down the names of the seventy-seven officials and elders of Succoth, we may gather that writing was a common accomplishment. The Israelites owed their literacy largely to the simple Canaanite script, which was much easier to learn than Egyptian hieroglyphs and Mesopotamian syllabic cuneiform writing. While the other inhabitants of Palestine, too, knew how to write, the Israelites alone endowed their stories with what for the time was a unique historical consciousness.

Their inability to consolidate the bond between them was responsible for the defeat of the tribes of Israel at Aphek, described in 1 Sam. 4. The Bible associates this catastrophic event with the story of the Ark which was kept at Shiloh, where Eli and his sons Hophni and Phinehas (names of

Egyptian origin) officiated as priests.[1] From this narrative
we know that the Ark had not disappeared during the turbulent era of the Judges. In the decisive defeat of Israel at
Aphek, the Ark was captured by the victorious Philistines.
The sons of Eli were slain on the battlefield and Eli himself
died when he received the terrible news. Excavations by
Danish archaeologists at Seilun have corroborated the story
of Shiloh's destruction. The effects of this national catastrophe were so lasting that even Jeremiah still harked back to
it (Jer. 7: 12 and 15; 26: 6 and 9). The defeat might have
spelled the end of Israel's national and religious existence,
had not Eli's servant, the young Samuel, grown up in the
shadow of the Temple of Shiloh. Samuel, more than any
previous judge, steered his people's ship safely through the
storm.

[1] Phinehas was also the name of Aaron's grandson (Exod. 6: 25).
It means "the Nubian" and is used in Egyptian texts from 1550 B.C.
onwards. "Hophni" is probably derived from the Egyptian *hfnw* meaning "tadpole."

VI

SAMUEL AND SAUL

At a time when the Philistines ruled over all central Palestine (in the eleventh century B.C.), Samuel paved the way for the future kingdom by uniting the tribes of Israel throughout the country. The Bible tells us very little about the person and work of this most important of all the judges. The first book of Samuel begins with an account of how the young Samuel was taken to Shiloh, to serve under Eli who was both priest and judge. From the description of the temple and the sacrificial rites in Shiloh we learn that sacrificial flesh had to be boiled in a pot, and that the priest was allowed to keep for himself what his fleshhook brought forth from it. Eli's sons sinned against this custom by cutting off the best pieces of the flesh before putting it into the pot, thus betraying their trust. In this way it was made clear why the priesthood was taken away from the house of Eli.

Having described Shiloh's fall, the Biblical narrator turns to the fate of the Ark which the Philistines had captured.[1] Since the Ark caused havoc in the Philistine cities to which it was taken, the Philistines decided to restore it to Israel, by way of Ashdod. The first Israelite town reached was Beth-

[1] There is a clear distinction between the Ark and the Tabernacle which, according to 2 Chron. 1 : 3, stood on a hill in Gibeon. In 1 Chron. 21 : 29 we are told that not only the Tabernacle, which Moses had made in the wilderness, but also the altar of the burnt offering was kept on that hill.

shemesh, some of the inhabitants of which allowed their curiosity to get the better of them so that they looked into the Ark (1 Sam. 6: 19). For this sin they were stricken down by a plague. Thereupon the Ark was taken to Kirjath-jearim, which was nearer to Jerusalem—then as yet a Canaanite city—and to the centre of the country. Only after he has described the fate of the Ark does the Biblical author return to Samuel himself.

We are told that Samuel dispensed justice to his people from Ramah, where he had built an altar unto the Lord. He had earned the reputation of being a great "seer." He could, for instance, find lost property, and thus it came about that Saul turned to him when he had lost his father's asses (1 Sam. 9: 8–9). Samuel was present at only one battle: the victory over the Philistines at Mizpah (north of Jerusalem) in which Samuel saw a direct intervention by God (1 Sam. 7: 10), and in honour of which he erected a stone which he called Eben-ezer (stone of help). However, even after the victory, the area over which he was judge remained small— his circuit consisted mainly of Ramah, Bethel, Gilgad and Mizpah, all of which were right in the interior of Palestine. Moreover, the Philistines continued to threaten the people, so much so that the Israelites had to join forces with their former enemies, the Canaanites (called Amorites in 1 Sam. 7: 14), for their mutual protection.

While Samuel was judge, the people themselves expressed the desire for a king. Kings, unlike judges, were to be hereditary rulers. At first, the Israelites must have intended to turn the house of Samuel into a dynasty, and it was only because he was old and his sons took bribes and "walked not in his ways" that Samuel was asked by the elders of Israel to appoint another king "to judge us like all the nations" (1

Sam. 8: 5). Kingship represented a revolution in the life of the Israelites, who were not used to a strict central government, to a court, or to conscription, which a king, by virtue of his absolute powers, could impose on his subjects. The many objections to this step by a nation of free peasants, only just emerged from nomadic life, are summarised in 1 Sam. 8: 11–18. Oddly enough, the author fails to mention any danger of a possible deification of the king.

Samuel finally gave in to the elders' urgings and anointed Saul the king over them. Saul was the son of a respected family, so much so that the Bible saw fit to mention not only his father's but also his grandfather's and his great-grandfather's names. He was born in Gibeah, some three miles north of Jerusalem. In the ruins of *Tell el Ful* (Gibeah) archaeologists have found a rather primitive but solid fortress which must have been Saul's "palace." It was built on a hill and overlooked the road leading to Bethel, Shiloh and Shechem in the north, and relied for its water supply on cisterns hewn into the rocks. Gibeah must have been populated in about 1200 B.C., and destroyed roughly one century after its foundation. Possibly the archaeological evidence of the destruction corroborates the events described in Judges 20, which tells of the punishment of the tribe of Benjamin by the other tribes of Israel. Saul's palace was built on the ruins of the destroyed city. It had two stories and was of considerable size. In its vicinity, archaeologists have unearthed bronze arrow-heads, stones for slingshots, an iron plough and other objects which indicate that Israelite life of Saul's time must have been fairly primitive.

Three Biblical reports mention Saul's coronation, 1 Sam. 9 and 10: 1–16; 1 Sam. 10: 17–24; and 1 Sam. 11. While the first report stresses the purely human factors that decided

the choice of Saul as king, the third explains his gaining of
the crown with his successful campaign against the Ammonites. An allusion in Samuel's address (1 Sam. 12: 12)
supports the idea that it was because of the threat to Israel
by the Ammonite King Nahash that a kingdom was established in Israel.

Since Saul's small army had to cross Philistine country—

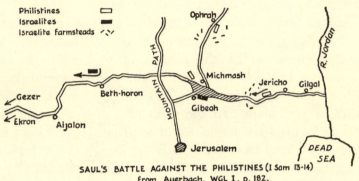

SAUL'S BATTLE AGAINST THE PHILISTINES (1 Sam 13-14)
from Auerbach, WGL I, p. 182.

even Saul's native Gibeah was occupied by the Philistines
(1 Sam. 13: 2)—to relieve the town of Jabesh in Transjordan from the Ammonite pressure, it seems likely that Saul
had the support of the Philistines in this struggle. Little did
they suspect what tremendous forces they were unleashing
when they encouraged the formation of an Israelite army.
After this campaign against the Ammonites, the Israelites
did not go back "each into his tent," but went on to Gilgal
(near Jericho) where Saul was proclaimed king. At that
time he was still a king without country, since, as we saw,
even his own Gibeah was occupied by the Philistines.

However the tables were turned on the Philistines when
Jonathan, Saul's son, managed to drive them from Geba (1
Sam. 13: 3). The Philistines took up position in Michmash,

Samaritan priests celebrating Passover on Mt. Gerizim

Top: View of Mt. Hermon from Tiberias
Bottom: Aerial view of the Jordan near Jericho

The Jordan, south of the Sea of Galilee

The Jabbok, dividing Ammon from Moab (Gen. 32:22–32)

The Wadi el Qelt near Jericho

Left: Excavations near Jericho. Note the white "gutted layer"

Right: Looking towards the Mount of the Temptation from the excavated walls of Jericho

Mt. Tabor

Bedouin in the Negev

The environs of Kiriath-jearim

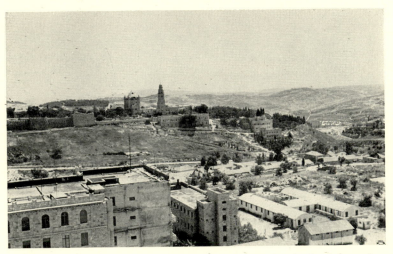

View of Mt. Zion with the Judean Wilderness in the background

Trough from Solomon's (or Ahab's) stables in Megiddo.
Palestine Archaeological Museum, Jerusalem (Jordan)

Mosque of Omar standing over the sacred rock which once bore
Solomon's sacrificial altar

The Gezer calendar, listing the agricultural seasons

A piece of Omri's wall at Samaria

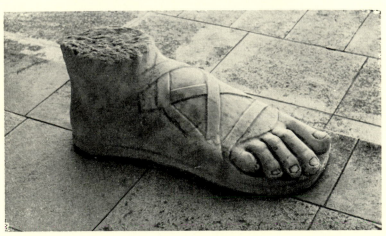

Votive Object. The Foot of a god. (See p. 101, note 3)

Remains of royal castle near modern town of Ramath-Rachel, South of Jerusalem. Possibly Uzziah's refuge (2 Kings 15:5)

Ostracon from Samaria inscribed during the reign of King Jeroboam II.
An order for grain

The Tigris flowing past the ruins of Asshur

The temple-gates of Asshur

Assyrian bas-relief being dug out from the ruins of Nimrud (Calah)

east of Geba and separated from Geba by a deep *wadi*. Saul's position was hazardous; his army had begun to dissolve and he commanded a mere 600 men. For a time the two armies dug in, but then the Philistines advanced in three companies and tried to encircle Saul's forces. In so doing, they left their centre exposed, and a shrewd counter-attack by Jonathan proved successful. The victory and its aftermath are described in 1 Sam. 13–14 at far greater length than the Bible usually devotes to military happenings. The report, originally written by an eye-witness, was clearly "improved" by a later author in order to explain the estrangement between Samuel and Saul. Hence it is rather difficult to reconstruct the actual events. Apparently, Saul exploited the enemy's confusion to pursue him far into his own territory. Covering some 25 miles a day with his men, he advanced west upon Aijalon, passing Beth-horon. Many of the Hebrews who had fought in the Philistine army deserted to Saul (1 Sam. 14: 21). Although Saul's men were exhausted (1 Sam. 14: 31), the King was determined to carry on the pursuit through the night, against the advice of Ahiah (of the house of Eli of Shiloh) who had accompanied the army as a kind of oracle priest. All these events can be inferred from the story of Saul's oath, and Jonathan's unwitting transgression against it (1 Sam. 14: 27–30; 37–45).

Everyone familiar with the terrain of Saul's campaigns in Judea, must marvel at Saul's and Jonathan's bravery and military skill. With only a small army, they managed to free central Palestine of the Philistines and to put heart not only into the Hebrews but also into the Canaanite peasantry. Isolated references indicate that Saul also fought against Moab, Ammon, Edom, Zobah and Amalek, though these campaigns were probably no more than border skirmishes.

Thus Saul became the soldier-king who owed his authority to military victories. He maintained the smallest of courts, in which his cousin Abner, the captain of his host, held an influential position.

Some scholars have suggested that Saul's reign lasted for no longer than one or two years. They base this opinion on a vague passage (2 Sam. 2: 10) which may be read as saying that Ishbosheth, and not his father, Saul, reigned for two years, and also on 1 Sam. 13: 1, which looks as if it has been tampered with.[1] The original text must have read "twelve years," for only thus does the rest of the phrase ("when he had reigned two years over Israel") make any sense. According to the most reliable chronological reconstruction, Saul must have been about 43 years old when he was proclaimed king.[2] Saul's downfall was based on a number of inseparable causes. The texts leave no doubt that he was of a melancholic disposition—in the words of the Old Testament (1 Sam. 16: 14–16, 23) he was troubled by an evil spirit and could only find relief by listening to a harp. Above all, Saul had no control over his temper—hence his violent attack on David (1 Sam. 19: 10). His mental troubles exacerbated his conflicts with the priests, at a time when the respective provinces of king and priest had not yet been clearly delineated. Saul was a strategist who wanted to seize what military advantages he could without having to bother about the priests' oracles. Hence he fell out with Samuel, with whom he had a number of dramatic exchanges (1 Sam. 13: 5–14, and above all 1 Sam. 15). As a result he became

[1] Noth, who is one of the proponents of the theory of Saul's short reign, calls Saul's reign an *episode*. *GI*, pp. 142 ff.

[2] Auerbach: *WGL*, I, pp. 176–177. For a comparison of the chronology of Judah and Israel with that of Mesopotamia and Egypt see P. van der Meer: *The Chronology of Ancient Western Asia and Egypt*, Leyden, 1955.

an increasingly isolated man whose plight is described graphically in 1 Sam. 28. Saul was forced to resort to means of contacting God, who "answered him not, neither by dreams, nor by Urim, nor by prophets" using means which he himself had proscribed (1 Sam. 28: 6). His wilfulness therefore laid the roots of the great human tragedy from which both Samuel and Saul suffered so greatly (1 Sam. 15: 34–35).

The estrangement between these two men, each of whom had done so much to liberate and to consolidate Israel, forced Samuel to retire to Ramah and Saul to withdraw to Gibeah. The Philistines were quick to exploit the rift between them and to strengthen their own army. They had every reason to be pleased further when Saul's jealousy forced the bravest of his captains, David, to join their ranks. The immediate cause of Saul's hatred of David was the song of the women of Israel: "Saul hath slain his thousands, and David his ten thousands" (1 Sam. 18: 7–8). The metre of the original Hebrew version stamps the song as an authentic poem of the time. David's great popularity was an obvious threat to Saul and his dynasty; hence the King was bitterly resentful of his son Jonathan's strange pact of friendship with David (1 Sam. 18: 1–4). Worst of all, the priests of Israel, led by Samuel, had begun to look upon David as their future king (1 Sam. 16: 1–13). Saul realised the danger (1 Sam. 20: 30–31), but his melancholy probably prevented him from attacking his enemies with the incisiveness of his earlier military campaigns. Thus he sat by passively while the Philistines strengthened their hold over Galilee and even made common cause with the Canaanites. Finally, the Philistines drew up against Saul's army at Jezreel, and inflicted a decisive defeat on him. When Saul, making a last-ditch stand in the mountains of Gilboa, saw that all was lost, he took his own life and became the first suicide mentioned by the Bible (1 Sam. 31 : 1–6). The Philistines then advanced as far as the strategic stronghold of Beth-shan, and fastened the bodies of Saul and his three sons to the town wall. From here the inhabitants of Jabesh, a town across the River Jordan, took the bodies and buried them in gratitude for what Saul had done for them when Jabesh was besieged by the Ammonites.

So died the first king of Israel. Saul's work, however, survived his ignominious death, for though he lacked an admiring court-historian, and though later generations remembered him mainly for the role he played in the life of King David, there is no doubt that Saul made a lasting contribution to the history of Israel. His campaigns had taken him to the ends of what was to become David's realm. The idea of kingship had taken root and his reign had kindled a feeling of kinship between the northern and southern tribes of Israel.

VII

DAVID
(*c.* 1011–972)

THERE are two traditional accounts of the causes which brought young David to Saul's court. According to one version, Saul, troubled by an evil spirit, sent out for a harp player whose music would soothe his troubled soul. His messengers then brought him David the son of Jesse the Bethlehemite, who was "a man of valour, a man of war, prudent in speech, and a comely person" (1 Sam. 16: 18), and who later defeated Goliath, the champion of the Philistines. According to the second version, Goliath is said to have been slain by Elhanan the Bethlemite (2 Sam. 21: 19).[1] The Biblical story of David's fight with Goliath is one of many typical legends about a bad giant and a shrewd hero whose deeds win him the King's daughter.

From the first moment of David's stay at Saul's court, he became a close friend of Jonathan, Saul's son, with whom he signed a unique pact of brotherhood (1 Sam. 18: 1–4). Soon afterwards, David went into battle against the Philistines, gaining the victories that were so highly praised by the women of Israel.

[1] In the Authorised Version, Elhanan is said to have slain *the brother* of Goliath. This change of text is based on 1 Chron. 20: 5, and reflects a later attempt to reconcile the two versions. Some scholars have assumed that Elhanan was a pseudonym of David's.

At first, after his flight from the court of Saul, David was the captain of a band of refugees who "protected" the people against robbers. Though the Mari Letters (eighteenth century B.C.) contain the word *Dawidum*, which probably means "chief," the hypothesis first put forward that "David" was merely an Amorite title, has since been dropped for philological reasons. The story of Nabal and Abigail (1 Sam. 25) gives us a fair idea of the life of such men and their leaders, and shows how much they resembled Jephthah's band. Though David always respected Saul as one of the Lord's anointed, the King's hatred eventually drove him into the Philistine camp where he had to serve his people's archenemies (1 Sam. 27: 1 ff.).

After Saul's death, David, who was a brilliant diplomat, managed to repair the damage to his own reputation. While a Philistine soldier, he had made a point of avoiding all actions that might have harmed Saul or his army. Now, far from expressing pleasure at Saul's death, he executed the messenger who boasted that he himself had hastened the King's end.

After consulting the oracle, David went to Hebron in Judah where the leading Judean families proclaimed him king. His first official act was to send a deputation to the town of Jabesh to convey his thanks for its great services to the house of Saul (2 Sam. 2: 1–7). Saul's surviving son, Ishbosheth, continued to reign over the northern tribes for more than a year. He moved his capital to Mahanaim in Transjordan, and his authority depended on the support of Abner, Saul's general. With the help of Joab, David gradually gained the upper hand over his opponent. He was helped further when Abner fell out with Ishbosheth, who objected to his marrying Rizpah, one of Saul's concubines.

In the end Abner opened negotiations with David, who demanded that Abner bring him Saul's daughter Michal, now married to another. If David hoped that by having children by her he would combine the glory of his own house with that of Saul's, he was disappointed, for their marriage remained barren.

When Abner, with a number of his men, visited David at Hebron, he was murdered by Joab. David expressed his horror at this bloody deed publicly, and wrote a lamentation on Abner's death (2 Sam. 3: 33–34). He even gave Abner a state funeral, and fasted and grieved for him, thus proclaiming to all the world that he had had no part in the assassination. Abner's death, however, was a heavy blow to Ishbosheth, David's greatest foe. Soon afterwards he too was murdered, and again David cleared himself of suspicion by ordering the execution of the messenger, who brought him Ishbosheth's head in the hope of receiving a large reward. After Ishbosheth's death, all the tribes accepted David as their legitimate king. Thus it came about that at the age of only thirty years, David was anointed King of Judah and Israel in Hebron, which remained his capital for more than seven years. Here he had a small harem, and his wives presented him with a number of sons, all of whom had to be considered as his possible successors. Though some of them—particularly Amnon, Absalom and Adonijah—played a large part in the history of David's house, none was ever crowned (2 Sam. 3: 2–5, and 5: 1–5).

The Philistines could not have realised how dangerous an enemy David, their former ally against Saul, would eventually prove to be. But David left them in no doubt about his real intentions when he drove the Jebusites from Jerusalem, and made the city his new capital. The walled city on Mt.

Zion was a strategic strong-point, towering steeply and formidably above the valley. David's choice of Jerusalem had an additional political advantage, for the town belonged to none of the tribes of Israel and Judah, so that no one could feel slighted by the King's choice.

In David's day, the tribes of Israel and Judah had not yet been united into one nation, nor had the idea of kingship taken deep root. Each family and tribe preserved its independence and none suffered another tribe to gain the upper hand. Only in times of external threat or war did the tribes usually join forces, to return to their old ways the moment the danger was past. This love of independence forced King David to woo the tribes not only with his valour but also with tact and diplomacy.

Jerusalem, in which David reigned for almost thirty-three years, was a fairly small town by modern standards.[1] The reason why its fame has outlived that of the House of David, is that David ordered the Ark to be fetched there from Kirjath-jearim west of Jerusalem.[2] On the way, an incident occurred outside Nachon's threshing-floor—Uzzah, who had put forth his hand to steady the Ark as the cart was turning a corner, was punished by the Lord. David looked upon Uzzah's fate as an evil omen, and decided to leave the Ark in the house of Obed-edom. Only when no further misadventures were reported to him, did he finally bring it to Jeru-

[1] M. Noth: "Jerusalem und die israelitische Traditions," *OTS*, VIII, pp. 28–46.

2 However, the recent excavations have shown that the walls of the Jebusite city were much larger than was previously thought. See K. M. Kenyon: *In Search of Ancient Jerusalem, a first account of excavations designed to reveal the early history of the site, III. London News*, Vol. 240, pp. 578–580; "The Holy City from today back to 1800 B.C.", *ibid.*, Vol. 240, pp. 619–621.

salem. Wearing a linen ephod, David danced before the Ark, which was brought in "with shouting and with the sound of the trumpet." Michal so despised her husband for this public spectacle that she became permanently estranged from him (2 Sam. 6: 20 ff.).

The Ark, the symbol of Israel's nomadic past, had at last been brought to rest. The God who had formerly roamed with the tribes through the desert, was now a God with a capital. Jerusalem had become a holy city, and even when the Ark was carried off by enemies, leaving the shrine of the new temple bare, indeed, even when the temple itself was destroyed, Jerusalem's former glory lived on. The sanctity of the Ark and of the Temple had passed into the city and Mt. Zion. Hence, David's decision to bring the Ark to Jerusalem had a far-reaching effect on the history of Israel.

David's life is described by two types of sources. Apart from fragments of annals, typical of all oriental court histories of the time, the Bible also contains an account by a man who, although he loved and respected his king, never succumbed to the temptation to exaggerate his hero's achievements. For that reason, most of 2 Samuel is a unique document in the biographical literature of the ancient East. Though the name of the man is not stated, it would appear that he belonged to the circle of Nathan the Prophet.[1] Nathan, who had direct access to David's palace, had a forthright and independent mind. Thus he felt free to reproach David for having brought about the death of Uriah the Hittite, whose wife Bathsheba the King had coveted (2 Sam. 12: 1–25).

From this biographical document we also know of other

[1] A. Alt: "Das Grossreich Davids," *KS*, II, pp. 66–75.

intrigues and tragedies that blighted the life of David's court. Thus we hear that Amnon, who had raped his half-sister Tamar, was so filled with revulsion against his innocent victim that he ejected her from his home. Tamar's brother Absalom, anxious to revenge his sister's honour, ordered his servants to kill Amnon during a feast. The ensuing blood-feud forced Absalom to flee to Geshur, and it was only through the intercession of Joab and a wise woman from Tekoah that David eventually allowed him to return to Jerusalem. Through Amnon's death, Absalom had become David's heir, impatient to seize power even while his father was still alive.

Absalom tried to dazzle the people by his own impressive appearance and by a show of great pomp. He rode on horses, while David stuck to the far less impressive donkeys and mules. Moreover, Absalom considered himself to be a better judge than David. To further his aims, he made common cause with all those courtiers whom David had offended in the course of his reign. David sat by impassively as Absalom plotted against him, and only sprang into action when Absalom felt strong enough to have himself crowned king in Hebron, the former royal city of Judah (2 Sam. 15: 10–12).

David's first step was to withdraw from Jerusalem, and to prepare for battle with the usurper in Transjordan. Meanwhile, Absalom took public possession of his father's harem, and therewith proclaimed that the power had passed to him. Absalom's fortunes were reversed, however, when he listened to the false counsel of Hushai, whose glib tongue apparently refuted the sound strategic arguments of Ahitophel, Absalom's loyal supporter. The story of Hushai's deceit is one of the most dramatic in the entire Old Testament (2 Sam. 16: 15–23). Thus, while Absalom followed Hushai's advice,

David found time to reorganise his army, and Joab was able to gain victory over Absalom's army. Absalom was put to flight, his long hair was caught in the branches of a tree, and he was killed by Joab.

Absalom's threat to David's throne had been very grave indeed, particularly since many of the common people were deeply dissatisfied with David's reign. Nor was Absalom's the only uprising against the King. Thus we learn that the party of Sheba the Benjaminite rebelled against David, and that Joab had Sheba killed by the people of Abel. We are also told that, when David, in order to take stock of his forces, ordered a census, a number of tribes rose up against him because they—just like modern nomads—looked upon all public counts as encroachments upon their divinely ordained freedom. Joab seems to have been more aware than David of the ill-feelings the census would cause (2 Sam. 24). All in all, it is not surprising that David hired a guard of foreign mercenaries, the Cherethites and Pelethites, who followed their King through thick and thin. Their names suggest that they must have been Cretans and Philistines. The soldiers of the bodyguard, 600 in number, were recruited at Gath. They were commanded by Ittai the "Gittite," i.e. man from Gath (2 Sam. 15: 18–19), who in turn served under Benaiah. As foreigners, the guardsmen had little contact with the population, and hence were unlikely to be involved in domestic conspiracies. They were completely dependent on the King, whom alone they served.

David accomplished the task of building what was, for the times, a fairly large state, and of setting up the necessary state machinery with great skill. From the offices listed in 2 Sam. 8: 16–18 and 20: 23–25, we learn how largely he modelled himself on the Egyptians. Joab and Benaiah were in charge of the army; Jehoshaphat was a kind of master of ceremonies who supervised royal receptions and visits; and Sheva (also called Seraiah and Shavsa) was in charge of the records (his sons were later to become Solomon's scribes). The fact that the scribe's name was written in different ways, suggests that he was of foreign origin. This is also borne out by the name of one of Sheva's sons, viz. Eli-horeph (my god is Horeph), for Horeph was an Egyptian god. What David's government lacked was a dignitary who was "over the King's house," an Egyptian title once borne by Joseph (Gen. 41 : 40) and used again by Solomon's chief minister.

In addition, David set up a Council of Thirty, a body of distinguished men whose feats of war had been recorded in the annals (for instance in 2 Sam. 23 : 8–23). The priesthood was headed by Zadok and Abiathar, who quarrelled and distrusted each other. When Solomon became king, he deposed Abiathar, thus putting a stop to disturbances during the temple services. David himself lived at peace with his priesthood. He could perform the office of priest and consult the oracle directly, and some of his sons did likewise. Quite possibly Ps. 110 : 4 is an attempt to base David's claims to the priesthood on those of Melchizedek. In that case, David was considered the legal successor of the priest-kings who governed Jerusalem before the Israelite conquest.

The wars which David fought with seasonal regularity (2 Sam. 11 : 1) were generally successful. His greatest victory was that over Hadadezer of Aram, at a time when King Asshur-rabi II's Assyrian empire was threatened by the advancing Aramaeans. By defeating the King of Aram, David may well have saved Assyria from certain collapse. In any case, at the end of David's reign, Israel had become the strongest country between Egypt and Assyria.[1] It is therefore surprising that there are no extra-Biblical references to David's victories or, indeed, to David himself, and that archaeological investigations in Jerusalem have failed to reveal any traces of David's great works. We know that he used Phoenician labourers to build his palace, but that no solid temple was erected in his day, for the Ark continued to be sheltered in a holy tent. While an older tradition maintains that David had shed too much blood to be deemed worthy of building a temple, the Book of Chronicles asserts that the building of the temple was one of David's greatest ambitions, in which he was thwarted by external circumstances alone (1 Chron. 22: 6 ff.).

There is no doubt that David was an unusually talented man [2] and a fine musician. Though the Bible calls the string instrument he played a harp, it was, in fact, a type of lyre, of the kind depicted on a Meggido vase dating from about 1000 B.C. With his lyre, David would accompany traditional and contemporary songs, and also psalms that he had written himself. In form, idiom and symbolism, many of these songs, recorded in the Book of Psalms, resemble Babylonian and Assyrian songs, and also the religious poetry of the Canaanites, on which the discovery of the Ugarit (Ras-Shamra) texts (fourteenth century B.C.) has recently thrown much light.[3] The purely formal aspects of this type of traditional poetry were, however, transformed by David, who infused the spirit of Israel's religion into them. Thus David's

---

[1] A. Alt: "Das Grossreich Davids," *KS*, II, pp. 66–75.

[2] For the demonic aspects of the great love and friendship surrounding David's person, see Margarete Susman: *Deutung biblischer Gestalten*, Zürich, 1955, p. 116 f.

[3] Cf. C. H. Gordon: *Ugaritic Literature—a comprehensive translation of the poetic and Prose Texts*, Rome, 1949.

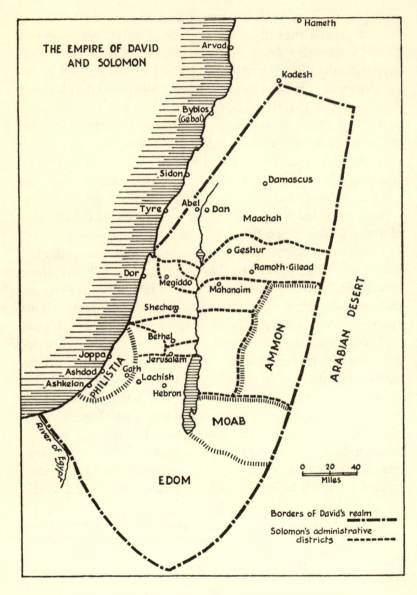

THE EMPIRE OF DAVID
AND SOLOMON

Hameth

Arvad

Byblos
(Gebal)

Sidon

Tyre

Abel

Dan

Kadesh

Damascus

Maachah

Geshur

Ramoth-Gilead

Dor

Megiddo

Mahanaim

Shechem

Bethel

Joppa

Jerusalem

Ashdod

Gath

Ashkelon

Lachish

Hebron

PHILISTIA

River of Egypt

MOAB

EDOM

AMMON

ARABIAN DESERT

0   20   40
Miles

Borders of David's realm ——·——·——

Solomon's administrative
districts - - - - - - - -

78

reign [1] is remembered both in song and story, two forms of artistic impression in which the children of Israel greatly excelled their neighbours. By contrast, Israel's contribution to the plastic arts was quite negligible.

[1] According to Van der Meer's chronology, (see Ch. VI, v. 4), David reigned from *c.* 1011–972 B.C. This view, which is borne out by what we know of the chronology of the Assyrian kings reigning at the same time and also by the so-called Regency years, has been adopted in this book. Very complicated problems are involved.

VIII

SOLOMON (971–932 B.C.)

THE Bible depicts Solomon, the son of David and
Bathsheba, as having been a far less colourful and vital
person than his father. The fault may have been his biogra-
phers rather than his own, for, unlike David, Solomon
caused few human conflicts and tragedies and hence attracted
much less notice. He came to the throne at the age of
twenty-five years, and reigned over the twelve tribes of
Judah and Israel for forty years. Though his personal history was rather undramatic, he, too, owed his crown to a
palace intrigue (1 Kings 1 : 11–40).

In the ancient East, changes of rulers usually led to
political disturbances. Hence a dangerous situation might
easily have developed after the death of David who, though
a popular hero, had never been able to convince his people
fully of the advantages of a hereditary monarchy. No
wonder then that various pretenders laid claim to David's
throne, and that Israel's foreign subjects sought to regain
their independence. This confused period is reflected in the
early annals of Solomon's reign, which portray the King as
a weak military leader, but as a shrewd politician. He
ordered the assassination of David's son Adonijah, whose
only sin it was to have asked Bathsheba to sponsor his court-
ship of Abishag. This "crime" seems trivial, until we realise
that claims to any member of a deceased king's harem—

and Abishag had "cherished David in his old age"—were tantamount to laying claim to the throne itself. Absalom, too, had tried to step into David's shoes by his ostentatious entry into his father's harem. Hence Adonijah's request gave Solomon a legitimate excuse to get rid of a possible rival.

Not only Adonijah, but also Joab, David's trusted general, and Shimei, a faithful supporter of Saul's dynasty, were put to death; Abiathar was deprived of his priesthood and banished to his own fields in Anathoth. In accordance with royal custom, no reasons were given for these drastic steps. Solomon was an absolute ruler who was free to accept or reject the advice of his councillors.

In his attitude towards neighbouring countries, Solomon was far less ruthless. Unlike his father, he waged no expansionist wars, and he restricted his campaigns to fighting those enemies who threatened his own territory. One of these was Hadad the Edomite, who returned from Egyptian exile as soon as he heard of David's death, to become Solomon's great adversary. But Solomon simply kept control over the desert route through the Arabah valley to the Red Sea, leaving Hadad free to roam east of the valley.

Another threat to Solomon came from Rezon, the son of Eliada, a former bandit chief, who now called himself king of Damascus. Though Rezon eventually plagued the northern tribes of Israel, Solomon sent no punitive expedition against him (1 Kings 11 : 23).

Solomon's relations with King Hiram of Tyre seemed friendly enough, for Tyre readily supplied the wood which King Solomon needed for his building projects. However, Hiram extracted what must have been extortionate payment, since we are told—quite by the way—that Solomon was forced to cede almost the whole of Galilee to him (1 Kings

9 : 10–14). It seems unlikely that Solomon surrendered so considerable an area without qualms, but in any case, he preferred this kind of settlement to the battlefield. The only new territory Solomon acquired came to him through his marriage to a Pharaoh's daughter—his father-in-law captured the fortified city of Gezer, on the border between the mountains and the Philistine coastline, and presented it to him.

Although David's great empire had shrunk in size and prestige under his successor, Solomon managed to store up vast treasures in Jerusalem. His wealth was based not on booty but on trade. Two of the most important caravan routes ran through Palestine: the road from Mesopotamia and Damascus to Egypt, and the road from Arabia to Damascus. The latter also had a branch which led to Egypt through Gaza. By the eleventh century B.C., the camel had been tamed and had become an indispensable means of transport. With animals that can go without water for three days, deserts could be crossed far more easily than hitherto, and caravan routes were being used to an ever greater extent. Thanks to his father's conquests, Solomon had the means of keeping them safe, and of imposing a levy on all goods crossing his realm. Since customs duties in the ancient East were extortionate, Solomon's coffers swelled rapidly. In addition, Solomon took to trading on his own account, selling horses from Asia Minor to Egypt, and Egyptian chariots to the north. Eventually, Solomon's profit in horses and chariots was so great that he was forced to build such "chariot cities" as Megiddo, a fortress north of Mt. Carmel which controlled both the mountain passes and the northern plain. Though American archaeologists have excavated the remnants of Solomon's stables at Megiddo (now Tell el-

Muteselim), the ruins have weathered so badly that the modern visitor needs much imagination to form any picture of the original buildings. All those, however, who have stood on the hill of Megiddo can never forget the vast panorama stretching out beneath them, and will understand why so many battles for this strategic key point have been fought since the time of the Pharaoh Tuthmosis III.[1] Solomon also built chariot cities in Gezer, Baalath (also called Kirjath-jearim) and in Beth-horon—all as safeguards against the danger of Egyptian incursions, which did not apparently cease on Solomon's marriage to the daughter of a Pharaoh.

All sorts of hypotheses have been offered about the location of the mysterious and golden land of Ophir, to which Solomon sent his ships. We know that all Israelite sea voyages must have started from Ezion-geber, a port on the Gulf of Aqaba, for the only other serviceable port—Jaffa—was in Philistine hands. Ezion-geber, on the northern shores of the Red Sea, could only be reached from Jerusalem by an arduous journey across the Scorpion Pass and down the Arabah. The journey took approximately eight days, and the route is once again controlled by the modern state of Israel. When one looks down from the highest point of the Scorpion Pass on the desert stretching some 2,000 feet below, the modern traveller cannot but marvel at the adventurous spirit of those ancient traders who braved such dangers without any modern technical equipment. Solomon's men ignored the obstacles and were amply rewarded for their courage.

Excavations at Ezion-geber have brought to light many

---

[1] Tuthmosis' conquest of Megiddo in *c.* 1468 B.C. is recorded in his annals, carved into the temple walls in Karnak. Cf. *ANET*, p. 236.

objects not mentioned by the Bible, though they were essential to the survival of King Solomon's state. Furnaces for smelting copper and iron mined in the vicinity were cleverly kept at high temperature by utilising the prevailing wind. Nelson Glueck has drawn a graphic picture of the work of Solomon's miners, stokers and foundry workers, whose labours contributed so greatly to Solomon's prosperity.[1]

From Ezion-geber, as we saw, Solomon's ships set out for the mysterious land of Ophir. King Hiram provided the sailors and therefore shared in the profits. The ships went out for three years at a time and returned laden not only with gold, but also with ivory, monkeys and other exotic animals. Almost pedantically, the Bible tells us that Solomon's share from one expedition was 420 talents of gold (1 Kings 9 : 26–28). Since one light talent was equivalent to about 66 lbs., Solomon's share would have been 27,270 lbs. of gold! The imagination pales at so vast a sum, but even if the figure is exaggerated, there is no doubt that Solomon was an extremely rich sovereign. Egypt, which had thitherto had a kind of monopoly over the gold trade, must have been bitterly resentful. Later, Solomon's son, Rehoboam, had to watch his father's treasure being plundered by Pharaoh Shishak of Egypt.[2] It is surprising that, at a time when money came into general use, Solomon should have stuck to barter, forging his gold into shields for the House of the Forest, from which Shishak carried it off. The shields played no role in Israel's economy.

[1] Nelson Glueck: *The Other Side of the Jordan*, New Haven, 1940, pp. 98 f.
[2] 1 Kings. 14 : 25–27. Shishak's campaign has been commemorated by engravings on the temple walls of Karnak, Upper Egypt, from which it appears that he conquered all Palestine. 2 Chron. 12 : 2 ff. adds that Shishak—himself a Libyan—went into battle with Libyan, Nubian and Ethiopian soldiers.

But where was the golden land of Ophir? Auerbach's hypothesis that it was the Transvaal[1] strikes us as the most reasonable of all the many answers that have been given. The golden land was probably discovered by Phoenician sailors, who are known to have rounded the Cape of Good Hope. In later times, when King Jehoshaphat of Judah, following in Solomon's footsteps, tried to send an expedition to Ophir, the ships broke up in the harbour of Ezion-geber (1 Kings 22 : 48), probably because Jehoshaphat could not call upon Phoenician sailors and shipbuilders to sail and rig his vessels for the three-year voyage; one year outward bound, one year at anchor while the gold was bought and loaded, and one year homeward bound.

Large though Solomon's profits from these expeditions must have been, they failed to pay for the upkeep of his resplendent court in Jerusalem and for his considerable building programme. These costs had to be met by the people of Judah and Israel. Heavy taxes and compulsory labour were bitterly resented by a nation to which the monarchy was, in any case, an institution of doubtful value.

Modern scholars agree that Solomon adopted the Egyptian system of collecting taxes by provinces. This is borne out by 1 Kings 4 : 1–20, whose author pays far more attention to historical detail than any other recorder of Solomon's deeds. The passage, which is utterly devoid of the usual stereotype embellishments, gives lists of the districts into which Israel was divided and also names the governors appointed over each of them. Many of these names are patronymics, possibly because the writer of 1 Kings had to reconstruct their bearers' history from faded or mutilated documents, or else because the fathers of such men as Ben-hur, Ben-deker,

[1] Auerbach: *WGL*, I, pp. 270–272.

Ben-hesed and Ben-abinadab had themselves been well-known officials. Whatever the explanation, this method of naming the governors is evidence of the antiquity of the document in question, and hence of its historical value.[1]

The geographical description of the provinces is so accurate that most of them can easily be located. Only the third province (1 Kings 4 : 10) is difficult to place. Apparently the divisions into provinces was not based on the twelve tribes of Israel and Judah, for Judah was left as a single unit. The choice of twelve provinces was, in fact, based on the twelve months of the year, so every province was taxed for one whole month. The taxes must have been very high, since in 1 Kings 4 : 22–23 we are told that Solomon's provisions for a single day were 30 measures of fine flour, 60 measures of meal, 10 fat oxen, 20 pasture-fed cattle, 100 sheep, besides harts, gazelles, roe-bucks and fatted fowl. For simple peasants, this kind of tribute must have been an onerous burden, particularly since the provincial governors were entitled to ask for further contributions to their own larders. We can imagine how much the Israelites, formerly a loose association of tribes, must have murmured, and how they must have longed for their former independence. Since Solomon, moreover, fixed the provincial boundaries rather arbitrarily, his system of taxation meant a further meddling with the traditional way of life.[2] Again, whereas each Israelite had once been a member of a kind of democratic peasant society, Solomon's trading ventures introduced class distinctions which undermined the old customs under-written by God. In so doing he paved the way for the

[1] A. Alt: "Israels Gaue unter Salomo", *KS*, II, pp. 76–98.
[2] A. Alt: "Der Anteil des Königstums und der Sozialen Entwicklung," *KS*, III, pp. 348–372.

prophets who, far from being the revolutionaries they appear to have been, were in fact conservative advocates of the old order.

Quite naturally, the official historians tried to keep silent about the popular unrest. But even they could not gloss over the strong opposition to Solomon led by the Prophet Ahijah of Shiloh, who eventually proclaimed Jeroboam king over the ten northern tribes of Israel (1 Kings 11 : 26–39).

Meanwhile, Jerusalem had achieved international renown through Solomon's buildings. The town which in David's day had covered no more than a few acres, had spread far towards the north. Solomon had it surrounded with new town walls.[1] Of the height of such walls one may still get an idea by visiting the so-called Wailing Wall on the west side of the temple plateau, in the Arab zone of Jerusalem. Gigantic boulders, 26 feet long and 5 feet high, were laid on top of one another, fitting so closely that no mortar was needed to keep them in place.

From the Bible, we know that Solomon also built a palace in which, according to 1 Kings 11 : 3, he kept his 700 wives and 300 concubines. For Pharaoh's daughter, Solomon built another palace, and he also erected the House of the Forest of Lebanon, probably so-called because its halls of pillars resembled a forest.

Right next to the main palace, Solomon built the famous temple which, though not much larger than a modern village church, was nevertheless a great architectural feat for the

[1] For the archaeological reconstruction of ancient Jerusalem, see J. Simons: *Jerusalem in the Old Testament*, Leyden, 1952; and L. H. Vincent and A. M. Stève: *Jérusalem de l'Ancien Testament*, I, *Archéologie de la Ville*, Paris, 1954; II, *Archéologie du Temple*, 1956, III, *Evolution historique de la Ville*, 1956.

time. It took seven and a half years to complete, and when the work was finished Jerusalem was proclaimed a holy city. Unfortunately, archaeologists are not allowed to dig in the temple precincts, since the terrace on which the temple once stood now holds the holy shrines of Islam, including the "Dome of the Rock" and the El-Aksa Mosque. Mohammedan law prohibits excavations near these holy places.

King Solomon is remembered as a man of exceptional wisdom and as the alleged author of the Books of Proverbs and Ecclesiastes. Among the best known of the legends illustrating the kind of wisdom God had bestowed upon him at Gibeon (1 Kings 3 : 5–11) evidently were the stories of his arbitration between the two mothers claiming the same child as their own, and of the visit of the Queen of Shebah. Though scholars are generally agreed on Solomon's wisdom, they have not until recently appreciated its full range. They regarded his 3,000 proverbs and 1,005 songs in which "he spoke of trees, from the cedar that is in Lebanon the hyssop that grows out of the wall; he spoke also of beasts, and of birds and of reptiles and of fish" (1 Kings 4 : 33), as fables with a moral. Now, while animal fables can, in fact, serve a didactic purpose, the passage we have just quoted does not entitle us to claim that Solomon was a moraliser—he might easily have been praising nature for her own sake. Such praises abound in the Wisdom literature, for instance in Prov. 30 : 15–16, 18–20, 24–31, and especially in Job 38–41. True, all these passages are not entirely free of references to human life but we must largely agree with Alt that they have many similarities with the Egyptian and Babylonian treatises on nature as such.[1]

---

[1] A. Alt: "Die Weisheit Salomos," *KS*, II, pp. 90–99. The Egyptian

Alt deserves great credit for having called the attention of Biblical scholars to the Egyptian "Onomasticon of Amenemope." This work, which was written *c*. 1500 B.C., was a kind of scientific encyclopaedia, and was headed by the words:

"Beginning of the teaching . . . concerning all things which Ptah created and Thot recorded about the heavens and the things pertaining to the heavens, about the earth and that which is within it, about what the mountains spew forth and what the waters irrigate; about all things Ra shines upon and all that sprouts on earth."

There follows a list of the creatures and things in the heavens, in the water and on land, of divine and royal personages, courtiers and officials, vocations and classes, ranks and races in Egypt and in foreign countries, of Egyptian cities and the buildings within them, of the various districts, of different crops and the products made from them, of various foods and drinks, and of the parts of the body of oxen and the kinds of meat they provide. Though the Onomasticon has not been preserved in its entirety, the extant fragments contain 610 systematic descriptions.

The Babylonians, too, had perfected a "science of lists," based on Sumerian dictionaries. These were composed soon after the invention of writing—shortly before 3000 B.C. The Sumerian lists were famous for their systematic descriptions of natural phenomena, and when the Sumerians were supplanted by the Semitic Akkadians, the science of lists was extended and translated into what became sacred texts. One of the most important of these, known by the opening

---

work was fully published and given masterly elucidation by A. Gardiner, *Ancient Egyptian Onomastica*, 1947.

words as the Ḫar-ra—ḫubullu, contained thousands of names of gods, plants, animals, etc., inscribed on twenty-four tablets. Although we cannot say with certainty whether, and to what extent, these Babylonian lists influenced the Egyptian lists, it is quite possible that they did, since, in the fourteenth century B.C., east and west are known to have communicated in the Babylonian language and script.

Looking objectively at 1 Kings 4 : 33, we are bound to ask whether Solomon, too, did not intend to introduce such encyclopaedic knowledge into Israel. If he did, we must read a new significance into the Biblical claim that "Solomon's wisdom excelled the wisdom of all the children of the east country and all the wisdom of Egypt" (1 Kings 4 : 30). Solomon was also said to be wiser than a number of sages who are named, but who mean little to us. All in all, Solomon's fame must have spread far beyond the borders of Palestine, even though there are no extra-Biblical references to him. However, the period in question is poorly documented.

We have seen that there is some evidence of Solomon's desire to produce something like the Mesopotamian and Egyptian science of lists. Solomon strove to give his people cultural parity with their neighbours, whom David had impressed with his military prowess alone. Later historians, who were inclined to stress Israel's uniqueness and superiority, had no appreciation for these efforts. Still, no one can deny that Solomon used his outstanding talents to sing of the "trees from the cedar of Lebanon unto the hyssop that springeth out of the wall," in a lyrical voice that made the dull lists of his neighbours dry as dust by comparison. Because Solomon's praises of nature have moral and spiritual implications, his original purpose was subsequently forgotten. All in all, recent findings bearing on the intellectual climate of the ancient East suggest that we may have to revise our earlier views of Solomon. He was a man, not only of great wisdom and talent, but of great scholarship as well.

IX

THE DIVISION OF THE KINGDOM

AFTER Solomon's death, he was succeeded, in 931 B.C., by his son Rehoboam, then 41 years of age. Rehoboam's mother, Naamah the Ammonitess, was the only woman to have any influence at his court. The wives of kings usually kept to the harem, and rarely gained prominence or entered into history. The queen-mother was one of the few exceptions, for her name was thought worthy of mention in the annals.

Solomon's empire was already dissolving when Rehoboam was proclaimed king in Shechem. Edom and Damascus had regained their independence soon after David's death, and the rest of the country, seething with resentment at the high level of taxation, sent a deputation to Shechem to plead with the King for relief. Solomon's former counsellors supported their request, but the young advisers, whom Rehoboam had chosen himself, argued that compliance would be interpreted as an act of weakness. By agreeing with them, Rehoboam hastened the rift between north and south, for the ten northern tribes, henceforth known as "Israel," banded together into a state of their own which continued until the fall of Samaria in 721 B.C. In the south David's dynasty managed to rule Judah until the beginning of the Babylonian exile in 586 B.C. The boundary between the two states coincided with the northern borders of the tribe of

Benjamin, which remained faithful to King Rehoboam.

The northern tribes selected their kings much as they had the Judges. A king had to be a proven leader in the field and his election had to be confirmed by a divine oracle. True, those chosen generally tried to establish dynasties, but none survived for more than a few generations. Thus, the dynasties of Jeroboam, Baasha, Omri and Jehu followed each other in quick succession until the final collapse of the Kingdom of Israel.[1]

The first northern king (931 B.C.) was Jeroboam of the tribe of Ephraim. As supervisor over the gang of conscripts forced to strengthen the walls of Jerusalem, he had earned Solomon's gratitude, and was appointed "ruler over all the forced labour of the house of Joseph" (1 Kings 11 : 28). While Solomon was still alive, the prophet Ahijah of Shiloh met Jeroboam outside Jerusalem, and promised him the kingdom. As a sign of this promise, Ahijah tore his new garment into twelve pieces. Two of these pieces represented the two tribes that David's dynasty would retain so that "David my son may always have a lamp before me in Jerusalem" (1 Kings 11 : 36).[2] When Jeroboam thereupon became the leader of a band of rebels whose spiritual leader was the prophet Ahijah, and Solomon's spies got wind of his defection, Jeroboam had to flee to the court of the Pharaoh Shishak, who received him with open arms. After Solomon's death Jeroboam returned to his native mountains in

---

[1] Of the nineteen northern kings, eight were put to death by usurpers, one probably fell in battle, and one died in an accident. Of the twenty southern kings, only Joash, Amaziah, and Amon died as a result of internal disturbances. In Judah the idea of the monarchy had taken much firmer root.

[2] Noth: "Jerusalem und die israelitische Tradition," *OTS*, VIII, p. 37, thinks this means "fallow ground" and not "lamp."

Ephraim, whence the people of Israel called him to Shechem and proclaimed him king.

Jeroboam's Judean counterpart, Rehoboam, was doomed to impotence from the very start. His chief collector of taxes, Adoram, was stoned at Shechem as a representative of a hated regime. Rehoboam himself had to seek refuge behind the protective wall of Jerusalem. Apparently, Rehoboam had every intention of asserting his authority over the northern tribes by force of arms, but he was dissuaded by Shemaiah "the man of God," who made it known that the succession was approved by Yahweh (1 Kings 12 : 21 ff.).

The seventeen years of Rehoboam's reign (931–915 B.C.) were not as black as they appear at first glance. True, the King could do nothing to stop the Egyptians from carrying off Solomon's golden shields out of the House of the Forest of Lebanon (1 Kings 14 : 25 ff.),[1] but otherwise he was left in peace. Archaeological discoveries of solidly constructed houses from that period suggest that the citizens of Judah were fairly prosperous. Naturally, Rehoboam had to strengthen his cities against attacks from the north, for Jerusalem was a mere ten miles from the border. Ramah, Gibeah, Mizpah and Bethel were all fortified, as we know from excavations at the sites of the last three. According to a very credible account in 2 Chron. 11 : 5–12, Rehoboam also fortified some of his southern towns—including Bethlehem and Hebron—against possible Egyptian attacks.

Meanwhile Jeroboam reigned in the north. His first capital was Shechem; later he moved his court to Penuel and from there to Tirzah. The Biblical author was appalled at Jeroboam's attempt to stop pilgrimages to Jerusalem by

---

[1] Cf. B. Mazar (Maisler): "The Campaign of Pharaoh Shishak to Palestine," *Supplements to VT*, Leyden, 1957, pp. 57 ff.

erecting two golden calves at the shrines of Dan and Bethel. It seems unlikely that these calves were meant to represent God Himself, or that the story of the golden calf (Exod. 32) was interpolated later as a warning to Jeroboam. We know now that Hadad—or Baal—the god of the wind was portrayed as standing on a calf or a bull.[1] Jeroboam's calf, too, was probably no more than a pedestal, over which the deity was imagined as standing invisibly just as He sat invisible over the cherubim in Jerusalem.

Possibly the simple pilgrims mistook the real purpose of the calves and hence sinned against the First Commandment. In any case, the shrines in Dan and Bethel became the subject of grave disputes between King Jeroboam and the prophets who had appointed him king (1 Kings 14). Ahijah turned his back on him.

Since Jeroboam reigned over Israel for twenty-two years he was still alive when Abijam, and later Abijam's brother Asa, was proclaimed king over Judah. Both were sons of Maacah, Absalom's daughter. Asa fell out with his mother because she "had an abominable image made for Asherah" (1 Kings 15 : 13). He destroyed the idol and burned it at the brook Kidron. Asa's long reign over Jerusalem (911–871 B.C.) was said to have been his just reward for his zeal in worshipping Yahweh.

Meanwhile, the northern state was in turmoil. Jeroboam's son Nadab was overthrown, and all Jeroboam's children were killed by Baasha, a man from the tribe of Issachar. Baasha (909–886 B.C.) tried to subjugate Judah as well, captured the northern fortress of Ramah and strengthened its walls. Then Asa bribed the King of Aram to come to his aid and Baasha had to beat a hasty retreat. Asa destroyed

[1] Cf. *ANEP*, pp. 163, 167, 170 and Fig. 501.

the walls of Ramah and used the stones to build walls for Mizpah and Geba. For the first time, Judah had called in a foreign king to help her against Israel. When Ahaz, in later years, did likewise, he had a precedent to go by.

Baasha was no more successful than Jeroboam in his attempts to found a dynasty. His son Elah had reigned for no more than two years, when he and his entire family were slain by Zimri, his captain. But Omri, the army's choice for the crown, rose up against Zimri and besieged him in Tirzah. When Zimri saw that all was lost he set fire to his palace and perished in the flames.

Many years later, Jezebel was to remind another usurper, Jehu, of Zimri's terrible fate (2 Kings 9 : 31).

At first, Omri had great difficulty in asserting his authority against a certain Tibni, who reigned over a large part of Israel. Only after he had ousted his opponent could he consolidate his kingdom. At the same time relations with Judah in the south were greatly improved, and the Houses of Omri and David became related by marriage.

Chronology

JUDAH		ISRAEL	
Rehoboam	931–915	Jeroboam	931–910
Abijam	914–912	Nadab	910–909
Asa	911–871	Baasha	909–886
Jehoshaphat	870–849	Elah	886–885
		Zimri	885

X

THE HOUSE OF OMRI

With Omri's accession to the throne, a new era dawned in Israel. According to 1 Kings 16 : 23, Omri reigned for twelve years—from 885–874. After six years he removed his capital from the previous royal city of Tirzah to the newly built Samaria. Apparently, Omri used yet another capital—Jezreel, where Ahab later quarrelled over the vineyard of Naboth, his neighbour (1 Kings 21 : 1). It was in Jezreel also that King Ahaziah of Judah called on his ailing relative King Joram of Israel (2 Kings 9 : 16), and that Jezebel, Joram's mother, painted her eyes and adorned her head and looked down on Jehu the usurper from the window of her palace (2 Kings 9 : 30).

More puzzling than his change of capital was Omri's ability and need to keep up two capitals at the same time. Omri bought the hill of Samaria from one Shemer, and named the capital after the former owner of the land. We are not told whether Shemer raised objections of the kind which Naboth brought up when Omri's son Ahab tried to buy his vineyard. Naboth refused point blank on religious grounds (1 Kings 21 : 3). Shemer, on the other hand, may not have been an Israelite, and may have felt no religious scruples about selling his barren hill.

Excavations have shown that Samaria was built on virgin

soil.[1] Thus, when Omri moved his capital, he was free of any local traditions, and could do whatever his fancy dictated. Samaria must have been an independent city-state, for when Jehu had murdered every member of the royal family in Jezreel, he had to make a special request for the surrender of Ahab's seventy sons who lived in Samaria. Apparently the city had the power to refuse, though, fearing Jehu's strength, they gave in to him in the end (2 Kings 10 : 1–6).

Alt has suggested that Omri did his utmost to spare the religious susceptibilities of his non-Israelitic subjects.[2] These people, who may be lumped together as Canaanites, had always lived in the midst of the Israelites. The Bible calls them Baal worshippers, and it is quite possible that Omri, though not himself an idolator, proved tolerant of their beliefs. All the evidence goes to show that Samaria remained a centre of the Baal cult until Jehu wiped it out.

Omri is not an Israelitic name, nor is that of his son Ahab (father's brother, i.e. father's equal).[3] Omri was a soldier who was proclaimed king by the army, and may well have been a foreign mercenary in the service of Israel, and one who worshipped an alien god. This would explain why Yahweh's zealots, led by Elijah and Elisha, rose up against his house. For the same reason, 1 Kings 16 : 25–26 speaks

---

[1] See A. Parrot: *Samaria, hoofdstad van het Koninkrijk Israël*, Nijkerk, 1957.

[2] A. Alt: "*Der Stadtstaat Samaria*," *KS*, III, pp. 258–302. Alt's thesis has been challenged by R. de Vaux O.P. (*Revue Biblique*, 1956, pp. 101–106), according to whom the existence of two capitals in Israel—as in Egypt or Mesopotamia—did not involve two independent administrations. Moreover, Jehu was proclaimed king only after he was recognised by Samaria.

[3] M. Noth: *Die israelitischen Personennamen im Rahmen der gemeinsemitischen Namengebung, Beiträge zur Wissenschaft vom Alten und Neuen Testament*, III, 10, 1928.

of Omri as one who walked in Jeroboam's footsteps and did worse than any that were before him.

Omri's further history is not mentioned in the Book of Kings. As a result all our knowledge of the considerable expansion of Israel under this great soldier-king is based on extra-Biblical sources. The annals of the Assyrian kings Shalmaneser III (858–824), Adad-nirari I (810–782) and even of Sargon II (721–705) refer to Israel as the "House of Omri." Long after his dynasty had disappeared, therefore, Omri's name was still remembered by the Assyrians—a striking proof of the great impression his military feats had made on Israel's neighbours. The Moabite stone of King Mesha (discovered accidentally by Klein in 1868 and preserved in the Louvre) also mentions Omri by name, saying that Moab was for long oppressed by him until King Mesha triumphed over his descendants.[1] Reading between the lines of the Book of Kings, we gain the impression that Omri did, in fact, do much to restore David's empire.

Omri's son Ahab reigned over his father's kingdom for twenty-two years (874–852). He was married to Jezebel, the daughter of Ethbaal, King of Phoenicia. Jezebel shared her table with the prophets of Baal and of Asherah, two Tyrian gods (1 Kings 18:19), and persecuted Yahweh's prophets. Originally, a report of this persecution must have formed the beginning of the cycle of Elijah-stories, which now open with 1 Kings 17:1. In their present form, these stories have come down to us as part of the history of Judah and Israel; hence the introduction is missing, and the uninformed reader is rather taken aback by Elijah's sudden condemnation of his people in the name of Yahweh. Only

---

[1] *ANET*, p. 320 f. For a partial translation of the text, see also L. H. Grollenberg: *op. cit.*, p. 80.

later does Jezebel's persecution of Yahweh's prophets crop up in a conversation between Elijah and Obediah (1 Kings 18 : 7 ff.).

Chronology

ISRAEL		JUDAH	
Omri	885–874	Asa	911–871
Ahab	874–853	Jehoshaphat	870–849
Ahaziah	853–852	Joram	848–842
Joram	852–841	Ahaziah	841
		Athaliah	841–835
		Joash	835–796

Ahab is also mentioned in the annals of the Assyrian kings. We are told that at the battle of Qarqar, Shalmaneser III was opposed by eleven kings, among them Ahab of Israel, who brought up more than 2,000 chariots and 10,000 soldiers. These figures seem very large, but there is no reason to dismiss them simply because of that. On the other hand, the Assyrian historians may have exaggerated the enemy's strength to enhance their own monarch's glory.[1] The battle of Qarqar was not nearly as successful as Shalmaneser's historians maintained, for it had no serious consequences for those kings whom he is alleged to have beaten in the field. Oddly enough, the Bible says nothing at all about a battle (854 B.C.) which helped to keep the Assyrians at bay for a time. Instead, it concentrates on Ahab's battles against Aram. This indicates that Ahab must have withdrawn from the anti-Assyrian coalition and that Palestinians could once again afford to squabble among themselves.

King Ahab was finally slain in war with the Aramaeans and his death is reported as part of the Elijah-cycle and not

[1] *ANET*, pp. 278–279.

in the royal annals. We are told that Ahab went into battle in disguise, for Micaiah had prophesied a bad ending for the King. An enemy soldier then "drew his bow at a venture" and killed Ahab unwittingly. The Biblical report ends (1 Kings 22 : 38) with a clear reference to one of Elijah's prophecies (1 Kings 21 : 19), which is immediately (and inexplicably) followed by a quotation from the royal annals, to the effect that Ahab had built an ivory house and that he slept with his fathers (1 Kings 22 : 39–40). Now, the phrase "he slept with his fathers" invariably meant that he had died in his bed, and if Ahab was indeed slain in battle, this would be the only occasion on which the Bible used the phrase in a different sense.[1]

In the Bible, Ahab is overshadowed by the prophet Elijah. Elijah belonged to a community of prophets who lived as single or married men under a "father." His first appearance before King Ahab and before the delegates of the people of Israel was made on top of Mt. Carmel (where a monastery still bears his name). Elijah was greatly aggrieved that the altar of the Lord on the mountain had been broken (1 Kings 18 : 30). From Tacitus[2] and from archaeological discoveries[3] we know that Carmel had become a place of worship to a local god called Carmel and another name

[1] B. Alfrink: "l'Expression škbⁱ im abōtāw," *OTS*, II, pp. 106–118.

[2] Tacitus: *Historiae*, II, 78, 3: "Between Judea and Syria lies Carmel; this is the name given to both the mountain and a god. The God has no image or temple—such is the rule handed down by the fathers; there is only an altar and worship."

[3] M. Avi-Yonah: "Mount Carmel and the God of Baalbek," *Israel Exploration Journal*, 2, 1952, pp. 118–124 has published a photograph of a gigantic foot, kept in the Elijah monastery on Mt. Carmel. This foot was dedicated to *Zeus Heliopoleites Karmelos* c. A.D. 200 by G. Julius Eutuchas, a citizen of Caesarea.

which varied with political circumstances.[1] Hence it seems probable that Elijah drew the consequences of Omri's conquests—the altar which had been dedicated to Yahweh in David's time, which had fallen to Tyre when Solomon had ceded Carmel, and which had reverted to Israel under Omri,[2] was claimed back for God. God's judgement of Israel (mentioned in 1 Kings 17 : 1) coincided with the beginning of the rainy period, whence arose the strange water rite, described in 1 Kings 18 : 33–34. Elijah's appearance on Mt. Carmel was probably of no more than local significance, for we know from the subsequent reports that Baal continued to be worshipped in Samaria.

Jerusalem had meanwhile become the capital of Jehoshaphat, the son of Asa, who began to reign over Judah four years after King Ahab succeeded to the throne of Israel. In a report by a later historian, Jehoshaphat is described as a model of piety and one of Yahweh's most zealous advocates. He is said to have beaten the Moabites and Ammonites with no other weapons than songs of praise to the Lord (2 Chron. 20 : 22). The Book of Kings tells us that Jehoshaphat was on friendly terms with Ahab, and that they fought at Ramoth-gilead as allies (1 Kings 22). When Jehoshaphat died after having reigned for twenty-one years, he was succeeded by his son Joram, the husband of Athaliah, one of Ahab's daughters. It was during Joram's reign that Edom proclaimed its full independence (2 Kings 8 : 22). Joram died

[1] O. Eissfeldt: "Der Gott Karmel," *Sitzungsberichte der Deutschen Akademie der Wissenschaften*, Berlin, 1953. Cf. also K. Galling: "Der Gott Karmel und die Aechtung der fremden Götter," in *Geschichte und Altes Testament*, Tübingen, 1953, pp. 105–126.

[2] In "Das Gottesurteil auf dem Karmel," *KS*, II, pp. 135–149. Alt has emphasised the fact that Elijah repaired the *Lord*'s broken altar (1 Kings 18 : 30).

eight years after his accession to the throne of Judah and was succeeded by his son Ahaziah in 841 B.C.

Israel and Judah had once again drawn closely together. While Joram reigned over Israel from Samaria, his cousin Ahaziah reigned over Judah from Jerusalem. However, the real ruler seems to have been Ahab's daughter Athaliah, the queen-mother. The Omrides were now at the peak of their power, though the death of Joram, Ahaziah and Jezebel, not only caused Athaliah great personal grief, but threatened her own life. She had lost a brother, a son and a mother, and she knew that the Yahwist zealots had influential followers even in Jerusalem. In 841 B.C. she therefore decided to stamp out all opposition and gave orders to put to death all the remaining members of the royal seed. She controlled events in Judah for six years.

Athaliah would have wiped out the entire House of David, had not Jehosheba, Ahaziah's sister, managed to hide the boy Joash, and thus save her brother's youngest son. When Joash was seven years old, Jehoiada the priest gave the signal for a well-prepared uprising (835 B.C.). Athaliah was slain, and the Bible reports at length how Joash, standing by a pillar in the temple, wearing a crown and holding the Law of Moses in his hands, was made king, while the people clapped their hands and shouted "God save the King." The uprising had the general support of the "people of the land" (2 Kings 11 : 18); who, as the leading land-owners, were consulted on all important matters of state up to the time of the Babylonian exile.[1] With Athaliah's

[1] E. Würthwein: "Der 'amm ha' arez im Alten Testament," *Beitrage zur Wissenschaft Vom Alten und Neuen Testament*, IV, 17, 1936. The expression " *'amm ha' arez*"—literally "people of the land"—later assumed a different meaning. In Jesus' day it referred to "the people who know not the Law."

death, the power of the Omrides was crushed. A turbulent period in the history of Israel and Judah had ended in victory for those opposed to any reconciliation between the worship of Yahweh and the religion of the Canaanites. The spirit of Elijah and Elisha had triumphed in the north and in the south.

IN THE SHADOW OF ARAM

THE famous Black Obelisk of Shalmaneser III shows Jehu (or one of his ambassadors) grovelling in the dust and paying tribute to his Assyrian overlord.[1] The inscription mentions an Assyrian campaign against Palestine which must have taken place in about 841 B.C. Apart from Jehu, Shalmaneser's Annals also mention Adad-idri (Hadadezer), described as "son of a nobody" or "commoner," i.e. usurper, and his successor Hazael of Aram. Hence we may infer that changes of throne were no more regular in Aram than they were in Israel. 2 Kings 8 : 7–15 bears out this contention.

While they were all threatened by Assyria, the small states of Palestine made common cause, but the moment the Assyrians were weakened by internal dissension, the old feuds flamed up anew. Though Assyria continued to impose tributes on Palestine, as we know for instance from the Annals of Adad-nirari III (809–782),[2] the local princes felt strong enough to attack one another, and thus prepared the

---

[1] *ANEP*, p. 122. The text reads: "The tribute of Jehu of the House *Hu-um-ri-A* [Omri = Israel]. From him I received silver, gold, a golden bowl, a golden cask, golden beakers, golden pails, pewterware, a sceptre, and *puruḫtu* wood."

[2] "From the Euphrates to the Great Sea where the sun setteth, I subjected all Ḫattu and Amurru, the lands of Tyre, Sidon, Bit-Ḫumri, Edom and Philistia. I imposed a heavy burden upon them."

way for their final subjugation by Tiglath-pileser III (745–727).

From the Second Book of Kings it becomes clear that the reign of Jehu and his successors was blighted by the constant struggles with Aram, though, according to the Bible, Jehu's misfortunes were the direct result of his reluctance to destroy the idols in Dan and Bethel. Thus we are told in 2 Kings 10:32–33: "In those days the Lord began to cut Israel short: and Hazael smote them in all the coasts of Israel; from Jordan eastward, all the land of Gilead, the Gadites and the Reubenites, and the Manassites from Aroer, which is by the river Arnon, even Gilead and Bashan." Nor did matters improve under Jehoahaz, Jehu's son and heir. Time and again, Aram attacked, and though the Biblical narrator (reflecting the theological *Leitmotif* of the Book of Judges) asserts that Yahweh sent Israel a "saviour" (2 Kings 13:5), Jehoahaz' army was reduced to a mere fifty horsemen, ten chariots and 10,000 foot soldiers. So small a body of men could do little to keep Aram at bay, and it was only under Jehoash or Joash, Jehu's grandson, that the tables were once again turned on the Aramaeans.

The Bible recounts the history of that period against the life of the prophet Elisha. The Elisha story incorporates a number of deliverance legends that are difficult to date (cf. 2 Kings 6:8–23, and 6:24–7:20). From 2 Kings 13:5, it would appear that these legends were recited annually during local thanksgiving ceremonies, as a token of gratitude for God's help. Hence the historical basis of the legends received little attention. The King of Israel in them remains nameless, and if the King of Aram is referred to as Ben-hadad, this is not so much an identification as equivalent to King of Damascus. The effect of these legends on Israel's national consciousness was far greater than that of the actual historical events, for they imbued the people with a keen sense of destiny.

Although Damascus was far away from Judah, even Jerusalem was threatened by the growing might of Aram. According to 2 Kings 12 : 17, King Hazael of Aram, having conquered the ancient Philistine city of Gath, "set his face to go up against Jerusalem." Only when Judah had agreed to pay a large tribute, did Hazael call off his intended siege.

In view of the threat from Aram, it seems incredible that Amaziah, who became King of Judah after the assassination of Joash, his father, in 796 B.C., should have continued the war against Israel. All we know of Joash's assassination is that he was slain by his servants (2 Kings 12 : 20–21), and that Amaziah, his successor, executed the murderers (2 Kings 14 : 5). Apparently his victory over the Edomites went so much to Amaziah's head that he felt free to issue an ultimatum to Joash, King of Israel. During the ensuing battle near Beth-shemesh, Judah was beaten, Jerusalem's walls were partially destroyed and Joash returned to Samaria with gold, silver and hostages (2 Kings 14 : 8–14). Amaziah, like his father Joash, had to flee from his own people to Lachish where he was discovered and killed (2 Kings 14 : 19). He was buried in Jerusalem and was succeeded by his son Azariah or, for short, "Uzziah" (766 B.C.).

During the long and successful reign of Israel's Jeroboam II, part of which coincided with the first decades of Uzziah's reign, Aram was held in check, and Amos' pessimistic prophecies sounded like so many discordant notes. Amos, the prophet from Tekoah in Judah, who, not being the son of a prophet, claimed he was no prophet himself but only a herdsmen (*bōqer*). As such, he frightened the pilgrims in Bethel when, in the middle of the eighth century B.C., he prophesied war, destruction and exile.

Amos' sermons reflected his revulsion at the exploitation of the poor by the rich. The democratic peasant society corresponding to the Mosaic ideal had been destroyed when the economic revolution initiated by Solomon bore fruit in the rise of a merchant class which reaped ever-greater profits from a constantly growing market. The Mosaic law was formulated for an agrarian economy, and such institutions as the sabbatical year, the jubilee year, gleanings for the poor, the periodic freeing of slaves, the protection of widows and orphans, foreigners and Levites, reflected the needs of peasants. The only reference to trade was that divers weights are an abomination unto the Lord (Deut. 25 : 13 f.). No wonder that pious Jews were so hostile to the rising class of avaricious merchants.

Amos was the first of a long line of prophets, who were seemingly revolutionary but were in fact conservative upholders of the old democratic order of society. Amos chose Bethel as his main platform. When he proclaimed that Jeroboam would die by the sword and that Israel would go into exile (Amos 7 : 9), the priest Amaziah expelled him, for Bethel was a royal sanctuary or temple of the kingdom (Amos 7 : 13). Amos then pronounced a curse on the priest's house as well. We have no record whether it took effect, but Jeroboam II died in his bed (2 Kings 14 : 29) and not by the sword. Nevertheless, later generations remembered Amos as a true prophet, who fulfilled the prophetic demands of Deut. 18 : 21–22. In a time of great prosperity, he alone had predicted Israel's destruction, thus proving his divine inspiration. Prophecies that had come true in the past were looked upon as keys to future events, and thus as valuable tools in the hands of skilful seers.

Amos' gloomy prophecies did not, however, come true during the reign of Jeroboam, who even managed to exploit the weakness of his northern neighbours to restore the coast of Israel "from Hamath as far as the Sea of the Arabah" (2 Kings 14:25). Judah, too, took advantage of the political situation. King Uzziah resumed control over Solomon's roads to the Gulf of Aqaba, and fortified Eziongeber which he re-named Elath (2 Kings 14:22). In fact, some references in the Assyrian Annals suggest that Uzziah was the most important king of Palestine at the time, for he is called the leader of the anti-Assyrian alliance. Uzziah, who became a leper and as such had to live outside the wall of Jerusalem, entrusted all official business to his son Jotham. A signet ring with the inscription "Belonging to Jotham" was discovered in Elath thus confirming the Biblical report of Judean control at this time.

To sum up: the first half of the eighth century brought a considerable increase in power to both Judah and Israel. This period, however, came to an end with the campaigns of Tiglath-pileser III against Palestine.

Chronology

JUDAH		ISRAEL	
		Jehu	841–814
Joash	835–796	Jehoahaz	814–798
Amaziah	795–767	Joash	797–782
		Jeroboam II	781–753
Azariah (Uzziah)	766–739	Zachariah	753–752
		Shallum	752
Jotham	739–735	Menahem	752–742

XII

THE ASSYRIAN PERIOD

WHEN Israel succumbed to Assyria, she had already been
weakened seriously by internal struggles. With Jeroboam II, Jehu's dynasty had passed its peak—Zachariah,
Jeroboam's son, was murdered by Shallum after a reign of
only six months. Shallum, in turn, was ousted by Menahem
one month later. The prophet may well have been referring
to those turbulent days, when he said: "They have set up
kings, but not by the Lord" (Hos. 8 : 4) and "I gave thee a
king in mine anger and took him away in my wrath" (Hos.
13 : 11). Menahem kept his crown for ten years, thanks
mainly to the support of the mighty King "Pul" of Assyria,
whom Menahem had to pay 1,000 talents of silver, raised
by imposing a levy of fifty shekels on all the wealthy (2
Kings 15 : 19–20). Pul was none other than Tiglath-pileser
III, who was also crowned king of Babylon under the name
Pulu in 745 B.C., and whose annals record that he agreed to
spare Menahem's capital in consequence of the payment of
a large sum of money.[1]

One of the sad results of Assyrian oppression was the

---

[1] *ANET*, p. 283. The Annals mention *Me-ni-ḫi-im-me al Sa me-ri-na-a*
(Menahem of Samaria, together with Rezin of Damascus, Hiram of
Eyre, and a great number of other kings. Cf. A Alt: "Tiglat-pilesers III
erster Feldzug nach Palstinäa," *KS*, II, pp. 150–162. For an archaeolo-
gical account of the Assyrian period, see also A. Parrot: *Nineveh and the
Old Testament (Studies in Biblical Archaeology*, 3), 1956.

growing number of palace revolutions in Israel. Thus Pekahiah, Menahem's son and successor, was slain by his captain, Pekah, after a brief reign (741–739), and Pekah himself was killed by Hoshea, who was to be the last king of Israel (731–723). Pekah deserves special mention, if only because his actions are reflected in the prophecies of Isaiah.

King Pekah of Israel and King Rezin of Aram were agreed that the only way to stop the Assyrians was by a defensive alliance of all Palestine. Both kings had tried to persuade Judah to make common cause with them, and when King Ahaz, Jotham's son and heir, refused to comply, they tried to win him over by force (these events are commonly referred to as the Syro-Ephraimitic War—735–732). The resulting war has been recorded by witnesses from both sides—by Hosea from Israel (Hos. 5 : 8—6 : 6), and by Isaiah from Judah.[1] The latter tells us that when Ahaz, the King of Judah, got wind of the alliance between Aram and Israel, "his heart and the heart of his people shook as the trees of the forest shake before the wind" (Isa. 7 : 2). Isaiah—respected counsellor at the court of Judah ever since Uzziah's death—compared the two kings with "two tails of smoking firebrands" and instilled new courage into King Ahaz when he gave him the famous sign of Immanuel in the Lord's name.

King Ahaz thereupon repeated his predecessor's diplomatic game of calling in a foreign king (Tiglath-pileser of Assyria) against his adversaries. The Assyrian army had grown so strong that it seemed invincible. Damascus fell in 732 B.C. and with it the kingdom of Aram. Large parts of Israel, including all Galilee, were proclaimed an Assyrian

---

[1] A. Alt: Hosea 5 : 8—6 : 6. "Ein Krieg und seine Folgen in prophetischer Beleuchtung," *KS*, II, pp. 163–187.

province, and put under a governor whose capital was at Arpad in northern Syria. There were also large-scale deportations of the local inhabitants, whose land was taken over by foreign colonists.

All these events completely undermined the authority of Pekah. He was ousted by his commander Hoshea who, though an Assyrian vassal also, failed to satisfy his masters during the nine years of his reign (731–723).[1] When the Assyrian king Shalmaneser V, learned that Hoshea had tried to conspire against him with Egypt, and was refusing to pay tribute, he had Hoshea imprisoned, and occupied the land. No new king of Israel was apparently proclaimed, for the era continued to be reckoned from the beginning of Hoshea's reign, but the city of Samaria held out for another three years, and was finally captured by King Sargon II (721–705), Shalmaneser's successor. Sargon boastfully inscribed the report of his victory over the portals of his new residence at *Dur Sharukkin* (the modern Khorsabad) in large letters.[2] All we know about conditions in besieged Samaria is that, before it fell, famine had become so terrible that the inhabitants had turned to cannibalism (2 Kings 6 : 24–33).

The fall of Samaria was followed by a mass deportation of Israelites. The deportees were taken to the Habor, a tributary of the Euphrates, and to Haleh on the Tigris, where

---

[1] In the Annals of Tiglath-pileser we read: "Bit Ḫu-um-ri-a (= Israel) . . . all its inhabitants, their chattels . . . I brought back to Assyria. They deposed their king Pa-qa-ḫa (Pekah), and I made A-u-si (= Hoshea) king over them. I received from them ten talents of gold . . ." cf. *ANET*, p. 284.

[2] "I besieged and conquered Sa-me-ri-na. I carried off 27,290 of its inhabitants. I captured 50 of its chariots . . . I set my captain over them and imposed on them the tribute of the last king . . ." cf. *ANET*, pp. 284–285.

they disappeared from history. Their depopulated homeland was settled by colonists from Babylon, Hamath and Cuth (2 Kings 17 : 6, and 17 : 30–31).

When the stricken land was visited by a plague of lions, the Assyrians were told that this was because the new inhabitants did not know "the law of the god of the land." Hence they allowed one of the deported priests to return, with orders to teach the new population what rites were demanded by the god of the country. In this way, Samaria became the capital of an Assyrian province with a mixed population, which worshipped Yahweh, and felt itself bound by the law of Moses.[1] This led to the Samaritans' feeling of a national and religious separateness which was not disposed to yield to the claims later made by Jerusalem.

Judah, whose king had submitted readily to the Assyrians, had escaped destruction, though not subjugation. The Assyrians imposed heavy tribute, and Assyrian beliefs crept into the rites of ever wider strata of the population. Thus an Assyrian-style altar was erected in the temple of Jerusalem after the fall of Damascus. Ahaz had seen such a one at Damascus and had sent a model of it to Jerusalem with express orders to his priest Urijah to build one like it. When Ahaz returned to Jerusalem he found that his instructions had been carried out to the letter. He then set about making many other changes to the temple and the service, to please the King of Assyria (2 Kings 16 : 10–18). All these changes clearly reflected Judah's dependence on Assyria in even the religious and cultural spheres—a dependence which was to last for more than a century.

Ahaz did not live to see the fall of Israel. He was

[1] A. Alt: "Das System der assyrischen Provinzen auf dem Boden des Reiches Israel," *KS*, II, pp. 188–205.

succeeded by his son Hezekiah (715–686), who rebelled against Assyria and invaded Philistaea (2 Kings 18 : 7–8). He removed the most offensive images from the temple, including Nehushtan, the "brazen serpent that Moses had made" (Num. 21 : 9). Allegedly he also did away with the high places, stone pillars and Asherahs. He is greatly praised for all these deeds by the Book of Kings (2 Kings 18 : 1–8).

King Hezekiah's reign was one of the most critical periods in the history of Judah, whose territory was then limited to Jerusalem and its environs. This period is described in the Annals incorporated into 2 Kings 18–20, and is also reflected in the prophecies of Isaiah (Isa. 36–39). Isaiah and his contemporary, the prophet Micah, both gave inspired commentaries on the turbulent events associated with Hezekiah's reign. They had the good sense to realise that, appearances notwithstanding, Judah's hey-day was gone for ever. Isaiah's great vision (Isa. 2 : 1–4), which is repeated in substance in Micah 4 : 1–4, makes it clear that, in his view, Jerusalem as the city of peace could be turned into the centre of the world and the seat of the Lord, not by conquest but by Yahweh's direct action alone.[1] This view had important political consequences, for Isaiah preached a faith which—in theory and in practice—amounted to political neutralism. His: "In returning and rest shall ye be saved, in quietness and confidence shall be your strength" (Isa. 30 : 15), was King Hezekiah's chief diplomatic maxim. Meanwhile, a pressure group at the court agitated for war

---

[1] G. von Rad: *Der heilige Krieg im alten Israel* (*Abhandlungen zur Theologies des Alten und Neuen Testaments*, Zürich, 1951), has stressed the connection between these views, 2 Chron. 20 : 1–30 (the manner of Jehosaphat's victory) and also Ps. 33 : 16–18; 147 : 10–11.

against Assyria, and for an alliance with other powers, particularly with Egypt. Isaiah was an outspoken opponent of the Egyptian alliance (Isa. 30–31), and even walked barefoot and naked for three years, as a sign that the King of Assyria "would lead away the Egyptians captives and the Ethiopians exiles naked and barefoot, with buttocks uncovered, to the shame of Egypt" (Isa. 20 : 3–4).

But though Isaiah was against an alliance with Egypt, he was no advocate of reliance on Babylon, which had recently declared its independence from Assyria under Merodach-baladan. This King sent special messengers to Hezekiah, inviting him to take common action against the Assyrians (Isa. 39 = 2 Kings 20 : 12–19). Hence Hezekiah was constantly torn between the advice of his anti-Assyrian zealots on the one hand, and the prophetic voice of religious neutralism on the other. But though he vacillated, he did his utmost to reduce the Assyrian pressure on his country.

To prepare against a possible siege, Hezekiah fortified Jerusalem as best he could. He brought water into the city by a special tunnel (2 Kings 20 : 20) which was rediscovered in 1882 when archaeologists came across an ancient Hebrew plaque, the so-called Siloam inscription, commemorating the completion of this tunnel which—like the Megiddo water conduit—had been dug out from opposite ends. For a long time, the inscription (kept in the Istanbul Museum) was the only important text in ancient Hebrew characters.

The tunnel was probably completed shortly before Sennacherib laid siege to Jerusalem (701 B.C.). The dramatic circumstances leading up to this event are described in 2 Kings 18 and 19—two chapters full of valuable historical hints. We are told that Sennacherib captured Lachish, a much more strongly fortified city than Jerusalem. He commemorated this victory on bas-reliefs in his palace at Nineveh, which were rediscovered by Lazard and are considered the acme of Assyrian art. From Lachish, Sennacherib sent emissaries to Jerusalem to demand the surrender of the city and the end of the Egyptian alliance.[1] The Assyrian delegates made a point of not using Aramaic,

THE FAMOUS SILOAM INSCRIPTION

It was written by masons who described how they dug the Siloah tunnel from opposite ends, and how delighted they were when they met pick to pick. "Then water began to flow over a distance of 1,200 cubits, the rock above the workmen's heads being 100 cubits thick."
(Cf. 2 Kings 20: 20.)

the diplomatic language of the time, but of addressing the citizens in "Jewish" speech—the dialect spoken at Jerusalem —to make their threats known to the common people. They questioned the wisdom in relying on Yahweh for deliverance, pointing out that the gods of Hamath, Arpad and Samaria had all proved helpless against the King of Assyria. Their arguments greatly impressed King Hezekiah, who would have submitted, had not Isaiah insisted that Assyria's power would be broken from within. When this prophecy was fulfilled, Isaiah's authority became unquestioned.

It is very difficult to reconstruct the actual course of

[1] A. Alt: "Die territorialgeschichtliche Bedeutung Sanheribs Eingriff in Palästina," *KS*, II, pp. 242–249.

events, despite Sennacherib's own account of the campaign in the Taylor prism. In 1952, another prism with nearly the same text was discovered, in which the siege of Jerusalem is described as follows:

"As for Hezekiah of Judah, he did not submit to my yoke: forty-six of his strong cities, fortresses and countless small towns in the vicinity, I besieged and conquered by building earthworks, by bringing up siege engines, with the help of assault troops, by breaches in the wall, by mines under the ramparts and onslaughts with a battering ram. I deported from among them 200,150 persons, young and old, men and women, and horses, mules, asses, camels, sheep and cattle, in countless numbers. [Hezekiah] himself, I imprisoned in Jerusalem, his residence, like a bird in its cage. I surrounded him with earthworks, in order to punish the temerity of any man who dared to come out of the city gate. His cities which I had sacked, I took away from his country, and gave them to Mitinti, King of Ashdod, Padi, King of Ekron, and Sillibel, King of Gaza, and thus I diminished his country. To the former tribute which he was obliged to pay each year, I added a further tribute and the gifts of alliance due to me as his overlord. Hezekiah himself was so overcome by the splendour of my power, that he sent me at Niniveh my royal city, his Arabs and his excellent soldiers whom he had brought in to strengthen Jerusalem and whom he had received as a reinforcement—with 30 talents of gold, 800 talents of silver, precious stones, stibium, great blocks of red stone, couches inlaid with ivory, as well as state chairs inlaid with ivory, elephant hides, elephant tusks, maple and yew, all kinds of precious treasures, and his daughters, his concubines, and male and female singers. To pay the tribute and to testify to his submission, he sent his ambassador to me."

Since Assyrian annals were notoriously boastful we cannot trust all Sennacherib's claims. However, a matter-of-fact report in 2 Kings 18 : 13–16 states that King Hezekiah sent 30 talents of gold and 300 of silver to the King of Assyria and offered his country's surrender. A more dramatic kind of story, 2 Kings 19 : 8–13, adds that Sennacherib withdrew from Palestine on hearing a rumour of the coming of an Egyptian army. This report is confirmed by Sennacherib's Annals, at least if we read between the lines,[1] though the mention of Tirhakah is an anachronism. On the other hand, there is no corroboration for the brief claim in 2 Kings 19 : 35, that the angel of the Lord went out one night and smote 185,000 of Sennacherib's men. It may well be that this story was part of a Sennacherib legend, recited during the annual festival commemorating the liberation of Jerusalem. A variant of this miraculous story is also found in Herodotus.[2] Quite possibly Jerusalem was besieged by Sennacherib on yet another occasion, about which the Assyrian King's Annals are silent. The second siege might have been called off either because of an epidemic or else for political reasons. The latter seems less probable, for it was not until twenty

[1] Cf., H. H. Rowley: "Hezekiah's Reform and Rebellion," *Bulletin of the John Rylands Library*, Vol. 44, 1962, pp. 399 and 419 f.

[2] Herodotus: II, 141, reports that the Pharaoh Sethos had a vision in which the god Hephaistos promised him victory over Sennacherib. That night the Assyrian camp was overrun by field mice which gnawed through the armour, and the enemy was beaten. Mice as symbols of pestilence are mentioned in 1 Sam. 6, but there is no reason to think that Herodotus' legend was simply an elaborate version of the Biblical story. Both accounts are based on the historical fact of Sennacherib's sudden withdrawal.

years later, in 681 B.C., that Sennacherib was murdered and succeeded by his son Esarhaddon.

Under Esarhaddon, Assyria reached her greatest heights. Even Egypt became a province in 671 B.C., and may have been occupied by an army that was partly conscripted in Judah. It is therefore possible that the injunction to the King in Deut. 17 : 16, not to lead the people back to Egypt to increase his stock of horses, referred to the historical situation after Hezekiah. Similarly, the military colony in Elephantine or Yeb (an island in the Nile near Assuan), recorded on Papyri dating back to the fifth century B.C., must have been founded in the seventh century B.C., so that when Elephantine fell into Persian hands at the time of Cambyses' campaign against Egypt in 527 B.C., it must have been able to look back on a long history.

Assyrian supremacy in Palestine did not come to an end in 701, when Sennacherib had to call off the siege of Jerusalem so unexpectedly in order to suppress the Babylonian struggle for independence. Babylon was laid waste in 689 B.C., and for the next ten years it was deserted. This fact is often forgotten by those who question the validity of the prophecies in Isa. 13 and 14. In any case, Isaiah had been right to warn Judah against allying herself with Merodach-baladan.

King Manasseh (686–640) and his son Amon (639–638) are attacked by the author of 2 Kings 21, who blames them for having tolerated all sorts of heathen cults. Manasseh is also accused of having shed much innocent blood (2 Kings 21 : 16), and he was probably a leading advocate of syncretism. Clearly, this trend became more pronounced during Judah's political decline, when the gods of Assyria apparently proved mightier than Yahweh.

On the other hand, Manasseh reigned longer than any of his predecessors, and the Bible looks upon this as a special sign of divine favour. 2 Chron. 33 : 11–13 reports that when he was carried off to Babylon in chains, he humbled himself before Yahweh. The former idolator had therefore found his way back to God and to salvation. Manasseh's son, Amon, was murdered by his own servants (2 Kings 21 : 19–24 and 2 Chron. 33 : 21–25), and the "people of the land" had to rescue the dynasty by proclaiming Josiah, Amon's son, king, though he was only eight years old. With Amon's murder the Assyrian period in Judean history was concluded.

Chronology

JUDAH		ISRAEL	
Ahaz	735–716	Pekahiah	741–740
Hezekiah	715–686	Pekah	739–732
Manasseh	686–640	Hoshea	731–723
Amon	639–638		

XIII

RENAISSANCE UNDER JOSIAH

WHEN Josiah, the son of Amon, was crowned king in Jerusalem (637 B.C.), Assyria's power had begun to wane, though it was not until some twenty years later that Nineveh fell to the Medes and their Babylonian allies. But Assyria's pressure on Palestine had already decreased to such an extent that the anti-Assyrian party in Jerusalem grew bolder and envisaged the speedy liberation of Judah from the foreign yoke, and that Josiah felt free to introduce new religious measures during the tenth year of his reign.

His signal was the discovery of a book of the laws in the temple by Hilkiah the High Priest. Hilkiah had these laws read out to the King by Shaphan the scribe, and the King was so overawed that he rent his clothes and sent a deputation to the prophetess Huldah. When she confirmed that the newly discovered book contained the only and true law of God, the people went in fear and trembling, for they all realised that they had been living in ignorance of that law. King Josiah then called all Judah to the temple forecourt and made a new covenant with God.

Josiah's subsequent measures are described in detail in 2 Kings 23 : 4–27. Apparently, alien rites were being practised not only outside Jerusalem, but even in the temple itself, which was studded with vessels made for Baal, Asherah, the sun, the moon and all the other host of heaven. There were houses of prostitution for men and women, who wove hangings for Asherah; the entrance to the temple was decorated with horses and chariots dedicated to the sun; and on the hills outside Jerusalem there were shrines to the gods of the Zidonians, the Moabites and the Ammonites.

On Josiah's orders, all these abominations were destroyed, and even the altars at Bethel and Samaria were pulled down.[1] Moreover, the Passover rites were completely changed, and necromancy, wizardry and idolatry were proscribed. Josiah's most important measure, however, was to make Jerusalem the centre of divine worship. The priests who had previously been masters over all sorts of shrines, now became servants of the temple in Jerusalem.

The question has often been asked to what extent Josiah's book of the law agreed with the laws of Moses. Most scholars believe that it contained the essential provisions embodied in the Book of Deuteronomy. Josiah's law had lain hidden in a chest containing silver offerings for temple repairs. This chest was only to be opened when cracks in the temple wall became so bad that costly repairs had to be undertaken. According to 2 Kings 12 : 10, the chest had been put there by Jehoiada the priest as early as the twenty-third year of the reign of King Jehoash. Hence the book of the law may well have lain hidden for a very long time. Its identity with large sections of Deuteronomy is borne out by Josiah's attempts to centralise the Yahweh cult, one of the main objects of Deuteronomy. Josiah's other measures, which are mentioned in 2 Kings 23, were based on Moses' further prescriptions.

In any case, the so-called Deuteronomic Reform is clear evidence of Josiah's endeavour to shake off the Assyrian

[1] Cf. A. Alt: "Judas Gaue unter Josia," *KS*, II, pp. 276–288.

yoke. An independent religion and culture based on traditional precepts and customs had once again become possible.
Jerusalem's mood after the fall of the Assyrian Empire is best
reflected in the prophecies of Nahum, above all by Nahum
3 : 1–3, which gives a vivid account of the fall of Nineveh.
But though the "bloody city" had fallen, a new oppressor
was soon to cast his shadow over Palestine: the Neo-
Babylonian Empire. Against it, Egypt enlisted the support
of the remnants of the Assyrian Empire in the hope that they
might help her to keep the balance against Babylon. But
when the Pharaoh Necho took his army through Palestine
to the Euphrates along the well-known caravan route, and
tried to cross Mt. Carmel near Megiddo, he was opposed by
King Josiah. According to the Second Book of Chronicles,
Necho then asked Josiah to withdraw, especially since Egypt
had no quarrel with Judah. The Biblical author claims that
the Pharaoh spoke with God's voice (2 Chron. 35 : 21), and
that King Josiah was wrong to ignore him. According to 2
Kings 23 : 29, he was slain by Necho near Megiddo—and
borne by his servants to Jerusalem in a chariot.

Josiah's politics were neutral, with a bias in favour of
Babylon rather than Egypt. During the last years of his
reign, the struggle in Jerusalem between the pro-Egyptian
and the neutralist party had become sharpened. The
neutralists were unintentional supporters of Babylon, and
this was precisely the tragedy of the prophet Jeremiah who,
like Isaiah before him, advocated Judah's neutrality and
was therefore accused of being a traitor in the service of
Babylon.

When King Josiah failed to stop Necho's army in the
plain of Esdraelon and was slain, the neutralists managed to
proclaim his son Jehoahaz king, instead of Eliakim, the heir

apparent. Jehoahaz was captured by Necho, who imposed a heavy tribute on the country, and appointed Eliakim king under the name of Jehoiakim. Jehoahaz (Shallum) was taken off to Egypt where he was to perish.

Jeremiah urged the people to bewail the fate of this unfortunate ruler (Jer. 22 : 10–12).

Jehoiakim's eleven years' reign (607–597) had dire consequences for Jerusalem. The King and his party failed to appreciate the political changes resulting from Babylon's rise. As a vassal of Egypt, Jehoiakim increasingly incurred the wrath of the new power, which, under Nebuchadnezzar II (605–562), grew so strong that it became invincible.

Chronology

Josiah	637–608
Shallum = Jehoahaz	608
Eliakim = Jehoiakim	607–597

XIV

JUDAH'S FALL

WITH Necho's defeat by Nebuchadnezzar at Carchemish in 605 B.C.,[1] there began the period of neo-Babylonian rule over Palestine. Jeremiah's prophecies cover this period until the year 582 B.C., and his prediction that the reign of Babylon would last seventy years (Jer. 25 : 11, 29 : 10) was nearly fulfilled, at least in the eyes of his contemporaries: Babylon was vanquished by the Persians in 538 B.C. Since fulfilled prophecies were thought to have powerful effects, Daniel, too, used the number seventy in his apocalyptic visions (Dan. 9 : 24–27).

Nebuchadnezzar (*Nabu-kudurri-usur*) was crowned King of Babylon soon after the battle of Carchemish, succeeding his father Nabopolassar (*Nabu-apal-usur*) who had reigned from 625 to 605. As Nebuchadnezzar II, he tried to unite his people, the Chaldeans and the related Aramaeans, into one great empire, and his efforts were supported by many others of Aramaean descent, even in Jerusalem. Nebuchadnezzar modelled himself on the great Hammurabi, and tried to restore to Babylon, which had remained a holy city and a place of pilgrimage, the political importance it had lost. While we know that he succeeded in this aim, we have few

---

[1] E. Vogt: "Die neubabylonische Chronik über die Schlacht bei Karkemisch und die Einnahme von Jerusalem," *Suppl. to VT*, Leyden, 1957, pp. 67 ff.

reliable documents about his reign—the Babylonians had begun to replace clay tablets with parchment, papyrus and other perishable materials. From what little we do know of Nebuchadnezzar through inscriptions on buildings and public monuments,[1] he must have been a religious and artistic leader rather than a great general.[2] True, the Old Testament depicts him as a mean tyrant who destroyed Jerusalem and the temple, and who mercilessly deported the men of Judah, but the Bible forgets that Babylonian captivity was not the end of Judaism. Unlike the Assyrians, under whom Israel's traditions and religion were mercilessly rooted out, Nebuchadnezzar's "tyranny" was so tolerant that its "victims" were allowed to record his deeds in their own language, thus making them part of their own history.

Let us now look at the developments in Judah up to the catastrophe of 586 and 582 B.C. In 597 B.C., Jehoiachin (also called Coniah) was proclaimed king at the age of eighteen years. His father Jehoiakim had been pro-Egypt and had refused to pay tribute to Babylon. Shortly after Jehoiakim's death in the summer of 597 B.C., Nebuchadnezzar drew up before Jerusalem with his army. Jehoiachin, accompanied by his mother, his princes, courtiers and servants, went out to Nebuchadnezzar and surrendered the city thus saving it from destruction. Josephus reports that because of this sacrifice, Jehoiachin "is praised by all Jews in a sacred song."[3] According to 2 Kings 25 : 27–30, Jehoiachin was pardoned by King Evil-merodach (*Awal-Marduk*) of Babylon in 561 B.C. The thirty-six years which he had spent in captivity had

---

[1] The most important source is the *Wadi-Brisa* inscription from the Lebanon, *ANET*, p. 307.

[2] W. von Soden: *Herrscher im Alten Orient*, Heidelberg 1954, p. 140 f.

[3] *Bell: Jud. VI*, 2, 1.

not weighed too heavily upon him: he was surrounded by his family, had many children, and Babylonian documents show that he was maintained by the Babylonian King's treasury.[1]

Nebuchadnezzar's captives included all able-bodied men, craftsmen and smiths (2 Kings 24 : 16) and such leaders as the prophet Ezekiel. By deporting them, Nebuchadnezzar intended to weaken Judah's military potential, and also to prevent the emergence of a national leadership. However, David's dynasty was left on the throne of Judah. Mattaniah, the son of Josiah, reigned under the name of Zedekiah. At first, Jeremiah placed great hopes in this "righteous branch of the House of David" (Jer. 23 : 5–8), but in the end he compared him to the "evil figs which cannot be eaten" (Jer. 24 : 8–9). The dramatic relationship between the prophet and the King is described in Jer. 37–38. Jeremiah was accused of being a defeatist, and a friend of Babylon, and thrown into a dungeon, but Zedekiah had him fetched secretly to the palace to learn of Yahweh's plans for Jerusalem.

Zedekiah's attitude towards Jeremiah was influenced by the patriotic fervour of his court, which scorned Jeremiah's advice to keep the peace. During the fourth year of Zedekiah's reign, ambassadors from Ammon, Moab, Tyre and Sidon, came to Jerusalem to conspire against Babylon. However, Nebuchadnezzar's secret service got wind of the meeting, and Zedekiah was ordered to explain his actions. In the Summer of 593, he sent a deputation to Babylon, and Jeremiah used this opportunity to address a letter to the

---

[1] E. F. Weidner: "Jojachin, König von Juda in babylonischen Keilschrifttexten," *Mélanges Syriens offerts à M. Renée Dussaud*, Vol. II, Paris, 1939, pp. 923–935. The text contains references to *Ia'-u-kin* and *Ia-ku-u-ki-nu* from *Ia-a-ḫu-du* (= Judah). *ANET*, p. 308.

exiled Jews in that city. In it, he warned them not to count on a speedy return to their homeland, and pleaded with them, in the name of the Lord, to "seek the peace of the city whither I have caused you to be carried away captives, and pray unto the Lord for it" (Jer. 29 : 7). Soon afterwards, King Zedekiah must have gone to Babylon himself, and apparently managed to convince Nebuchadnezzar of his loyalty.

Meanwhile, Jerusalem was in complete spiritual chaos. In a vision, the prophet Ezekiel, who had been banished to Tel Abib near the River Chebar, saw how the temple was being desecrated by idolaters. Seventy men had formed a secret society of worshippers of Asherah; women were weeping for Tammuz, and between the porch and the altar twenty-five men were praying to the sun. This vision undoubtedly reflected the real state of affairs in Jerusalem in the year 592 (the vision is dated). Since Yahweh had apparently been defeated by Nebuchadnezzar, the people had turned to other gods. A time of syncretism, of religious dilution, had begun and the old faith had collapsed. Those who saw a guarantee of Yahweh's victory in the mere presence of the temple in Jerusalem, were scolded by Jeremiah (7 : 3–11), who reminded them of what had happened in the temple of Shiloh.

Nor was Jeremiah completely alone. He was supported by Baruch a scribe, and an official called Ahikam, the son of Shaphan, who saved the prophet from the hands of an incensed mob. Again, when Jeremiah was thrown into the dungeon, he was rescued by Ebed-melech, an Ethiopian eunuch, who obtained permission from King Zedekiah to save the prophet from certain suffocation. For this deed, Ebed-melech earned Jeremiah's gratitude and was rewarded

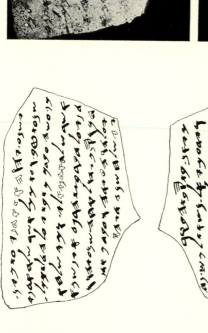

Ostracon from Lachish, from the time of Nebuchad-nezzar's campaigns. The conclusion reads: ". . . we are looking to Lachish for any signs my lord may give, for we can no longer see (the signals of) Azekah." (Cf. Jer. 34:7)

Elephantine papyrus (c. 495 B.C.)

The Nabatean royal tombs in Petra

Left: Fragments of the walls of Jerusalem in the Russian Church, near the Holy Sepulchre

Right: Imperial statue, discovered in Caesarea in 1951

Left: Walls of Herod's palace in Jericho
Right: The Sea of Galilee near Capernaum

The Wailing Wall of Jerusalem

The Sea of Galilee seen from the north

Decoration from the Capernaum synagogue (2nd cent. A.D.)

Entrance to the Royal Tombs in Jerusalem

A letter of Bar Cochba found in the Murabb'at caves

Letter written during the Bar Cochba rebellion

Coins minted during the first (rows 1 and 3) and second (rows 2 and 4)
wars against Rome

by the Lord (Jer. 39 : 15–18). Zedekiah's own attitude towards Jeremiah was ambivalent, to say the least.

In 588 B.C., King Zedekiah refused to pay tribute to Babylon. Nebuchadnezzar hit back at once and by January 587 (during the rainy season) he had rushed his troops to Jerusalem and sealed the city off. At one point it seemed as if Egypt was coming to the rescue of the threatened town, but no relief was sent in the end. Even while the King of Babylon's army was still fighting against Jerusalem and against "all the cities of Judah that were left, against Lachish, and against Azekah: for these defenced cities remained of the cities of Judah" (Jer. 34 : 7), Jeremiah prophesied that all was lost. In this phase of the struggle one of the ostraca (Ostracon IV) found at Lachish was evidently written. It refers to the fact that "the signals from Azekah can no longer be seen."[1] In July 586, Jerusalem surrendered.[2] One month later, one of its walls was pulled down, the temple and the palace were burnt, and 100 of the leading inhabitants were killed. Zedekiah tried to escape, but was caught in the plain of Jericho. The King of Babylon was encamped at Riblah, where he held judgement over his rebellious vassal. "He slew the sons of Zedekiah before his eyes and put out the eyes of Zedekiah, and bound him with fetters and carried him to Babylon" (2 Kings 25 : 7). A second contingent of Judeans was now deported. According to Jer. 52 : 29, 832 men were carried away captive, while according to 2 Kings 25 : 11 the entire population was carried off to Babylon. The second report is too general to be reliable.

When Jerusalem fell, Jeremiah was released from prison

[1] *ANET*, p. 322.
[2] According to some scholars 587. See e.g. M. Noth: "Die Einnahme von Jerusalem im Jahre 597 V. Chr." (*ZDPV*, *74*, 1958, p. 133 f.)

on the orders of Nebuchadnezzar (Jer. 39 : 12). Through an error, the prophet was included among a body of men about to be deported, but during a roll-call in Ramah, Jeremiah was recognised by the Babylonian commander and given the choice between an honourable position in Babylon or freedom in Judah. Jeremiah decided to return home, was given victuals and a reward, and went to Mizpah, the residence of Gedaliah, the governor of Judah (Jer. 40 : 1–6).

Gedaliah was the son of Ahikam, Jeremiah's former saviour. From Jer. 40 and 41, we gather that Gedaliah carried out the delicate task of governing Judah on behalf of a foreign power with rare tact and skill. From Mizpah (probably the modern Tell en-Nasbeh), he called on the peasants to return to their orchards and vineyards. It was Autumn now; the harvest had to be brought in, and the roving partisans who were plaguing the peaceful peasants had to be called to order. We may assume that eighty per cent of the original population remained in the country and that the Babylonians left a fairly weak army of occupation in Judah. Hence, though its leaders had been taken away, Judah was well on the way to economic recovery in the Autumn of 586. Gedaliah might have managed to rebuild Judah had he not been murdered by Ishmael, a tool of the King of Ammon. The Ammonites, Moabites and Edomites had all gloated over Judah's defeat, and were bitterly opposed to Gedaliah's plans to rebuild the country.

Gedaliah seems to have been a very trusting man. He turned a deaf ear to all warnings, and angrily rejected the suggestion of one of his faithful commanders to murder Ishmael. Instead, he received Ishmael and his entourage with open arms. Ishmael repaid the governor's hospitality by killing him together with all his courtiers—Jew and

Gentile. "They smote Gedaliah with the sword and slew him, whom the King of Babylon had made governor over the land" (Jer. 41 : 2). The Biblical report goes on to say that Ishmael's deed remained undiscovered until the second day, when eighty pilgrims from Shiloh and from Samaria arrived in Mizpah. They were on the way to Jerusalem where they were going to offer sacrifices and bewail the destruction of the temple. The pilgrims had shaven their beards, rent their clothes, and cut their skin, as an expression of their sorrow. Though the temple was destroyed, the holy places and the altar were apparently still open to visitors. Possibly a few priests had stayed behind to perform the religious rites as best they could. Outside Mizpah, the pilgrims were met by Ishmael who led them to the centre of the city with tears in his eyes and then had them murdered.

He may well have been afraid that the pilgrims would spread the news of his wicked deed, but his main motive was greed since, according to the Bible, he spared ten of the men because they promised him hidden treasures of wheat, barley, oil and honey. Ishmael believed them, for it was quite usual for peasants to hide their supplies from the Babylonians. The Bible hints that the ten men then made contact with Gedaliah's party outside Mizpah who thwarted Ishmael's plan, for when Ishmael attempted to carry off the defenceless population of Mizpah, including the princess, to Ammon, his caravan was attacked and the prisoners were freed. Ishmael himself managed to escape and to reach Ammon, where, for the time being, he was safe.

But the people had had enough of Judah, and made their way to Egypt via Bethlehem. They were afraid, above all, that King Nebuchadnezzar would hold them responsible for the death of Gedaliah. Before they left, they asked Jeremiah to tell them what Yahweh had in store for them. Jeremiah pleaded with them to stay at home and to abandon their journey to Egypt: "The sword which ye feared shall overtake you there in the land of Egypt, and the famine, whereof ye were afraid, shall follow close after you there in Egypt; and there ye shall die" (Jer. 42 : 16). The prophet implored them in the name of the Lord to continue serving God faithfully in their own land.

But they were too terrified to listen to Jeremiah, called him a shameless liar, and forced him to accompany them to Egypt. Subsequently extra-Biblical legends turned Jeremiah into a martyr. But according to the Bible his story ends with his being dragged off to Egypt to end his life there. As always Jeremiah was to travel along a path that had been chosen for him against his will.

Chronology

Jehoiachin	597
Zedekiah (Mattaniah)	597–586
Gedaliah	586–582

XV

BABYLONIAN EXILE

THE Babylonian exile had far-reaching social and religious consequences for Judah. In fact, it was in Mesopotamia that the bases for the later developments of Judaism were laid during 597–539 B.C. True, no more than twenty per cent of the population had been deported, but the remaining Jews had been robbed of their spiritual leaders, including the prophet Ezekiel. Ezekiel had been carried off as early as 597 B.C., and like Jeremiah, he had no expectation of an early collapse of the Babylonian Empire. Even so, he continued to hope for Jerusalem, and he drew up plans for the reconstruction of the temple (Ezek. 40–48) which were, in fact, carried out after the homecoming.

From the Babylonian exile dates a psalm which, for the first time in the history of the Jewish people, reflected a Zionist longing for the land of the Fathers. With the words "If I forget thee, O Jerusalem, let my right hand forget her cunning" (Ps. 137: 5), the Biblical author has recorded the fervour of Judah's longing for national restoration, and the symbolic meaning Jerusalem had assumed. The city which the Pentateuch had not thought worthy of a single mention, had become the centre of a people's religious longings.

Apart from Ezekiel's prophecies and Psalm 137, we have no means of assessing the exiles' real feelings. Some scholars have tried to infer the prevailing mood from Isa. 40–66,

commonly called Deutero-Isaiah, a section with which prophecies of Isaiah were brought up to date towards the end
of the Babylonian exile.[1] We do not consider it impossible
that there is a substratum of genuine Isaianic material in
these chapters. Hence Isaiah himself might have called
Babylonian captivity "a furnace of affliction" and said "upon
the ancient hast thou heavily laid thy yoke" (Isa. 48 : 10 and
47 : 6).

King Nebuchadnezzar had no intention of destroying the
exiles or even their culture. Probably the Jews—like the
Babylonians—were occasionally conscripted into doing public work, for instance draining the land or building dams.
While we lack any detailed information on this matter, we
have documentary proof that the Jews held important positions in Babylon. Thus clay tablets dug up at Nippur tell us
that a leading banking house belonged to the Jewish family
of Murashu.[2] The bank did a considerable volume of business, including real estate transactions. Since the tablets go
back to the fifth century B.C., i.e. to a time after the exile,
the Jewish bankers must have stayed on in Babylon of their
own free will.

From the Book of Daniel we know that the fall of the
Babylonian Empire cast its shadow before it. Nebuchadnezzar's heirs were incompetent rulers.[3] Evil-merodach's

[1] This "modernisation" of prophecies is borne out quite particularly
by the Habakkuk Commentary which is one of the most important manu-
scripts discovered in Qumran in 1947.

[2] *ANET*, p. 221 f. The texts were published by H. V. Hilprecht and
A. T. Clay in *Business Documents of Murashu Sons of Nippur, dated in the
reign of Artaxerxes I*, 1898.

[3] This does not mean that Babylonia was a stable state even under
Nebuchadnezzar. See D. J. Wiseman: *Chronicles of Chaldaean Kings
(626–566 B.C.) in the British Museum*, London, 1956. Cf. D. N. Freedman:
"The Babylonian Chronicle," *BA*, 1956, pp. 50–60.

reign lasted for only two years, and his successor Neriglissar—whom Jeremiah (39 : 3, 13) had mentioned in connection with the siege of Jerusalem and who must have been an old man when he came to the throne—reigned for only four years. He was succeeded by Labashi-Marduk, whose reign lasted for but a few months; Labashi's successor, Nabonidus, fell out with the Babylonian priesthood. He even absented himself from the all-important New Year Festivals and withdrew for seven years to the oasis of Teima in the Arabian desert, leaving his state affairs in the hands of his son Belshazzar. Daniel's vision (Dan. 2) predicts the resulting chaos: Nebuchadnezzar's kingdom of gold will be followed by one of brass, by another of iron, and finally by one of clay. In other words, the Babylonian Empire was a giant with unsteady legs.

It is against this historical background that we must read Dan. 5. When the ominous words appeared on the wall of Belshazzar's banqueting hall, the Babylonian soothsayers read them as names of coins of the realm—and could make no sense of them. But Daniel, inspired by the Lord, filled in the missing vowels correctly and hence interpreted the message as: "He (God) has numbered, weighed, divided." Thus Daniel predicted the end of Babylon, and Cyrus' victory.

The Babylonian exile ended the history of Judah and Jerusalem temporarily. When the people finally returned home, they found governors instead of kings and officials in the place of priests. Aramaic had gradually replaced Hebrew as the common language.

Unfortunately, we know very little about political or religious happenings in Jerusalem during the time of the exile. All we can say with certainty is that those who were left behind enjoyed the special protection of Nebuchadnezzar. On his orders, Nebuzaradan divided the land among "the poor of the country," lest the vineyards and fields fall into disrepair (2 Kings 25 : 11–12). Hence it was left to an alien ruler to remove the class barriers which Jeremiah had preached against so ardently. The disinherited had been turned into a class of yeomen (*am-ha-arez*) who must have looked upon the return of the former landowners with great misgivings.

By destroying the temple, Nebuchadnezzar had removed the heart of Judah's national and religious consciousness, and hence the symbol of rebellion.[1] However, Jeremiah's prophecies had prepared his followers against this event, so that they met it with equanimity and introduced new forms of divine worship, while holding fast to their faith in Yahweh. Others, however, adopted the religion of the Canaanites, for they felt that the God of Israel had abandoned them.

Those who, like Jeremiah, continued to adhere to Yahweh even after the loss of the temple, joined into a religious community which must be considered the forerunner of the synagogue. Though it does not mention this institution by name, the Old Testament gives us a number of hints about its origin.[2] Thus Jeremiah's letter to the exiles in Babylon, which we mentioned earlier, makes it clear that Yahweh was being worshipped communally even in foreign lands (Jer. 29 : 7). According to the religious belief of the ancients, communal worship was always superior to individual prayer, particularly on the Sabbath, a day which, since time im-

[1] Enno Janssen: *Juda in der Exilszeit* (*Forschungen zur Religion und Literatur des A. und N.T., NF, 51*, Göttingen, 1956), p. 47, suggests that the temple was first and foremost a bastion of the *am-ha-arez* who fought for Judah's independence.

[2] Janssen: *op. cit.*, pp. 105 ff.

memorial, was considered the most propitious day for consulting the Lord's prophets (2 Kings 23), or for offering sacrifices to God (Isa. 1 : 13 ff.; Lam. 2 : 6).

Then there were the three great religious festivals which, though originally associated with the agricultural seasons, gradually achieved a historical significance. These were days of remembrance of the great miracles Yahweh had wrought on His people's behalf. Janssen has argued convincingly that Deuteronomy embodies the basic liturgy of the original synagogue, at a time when historical gratitude to God had replaced the original faith in the immediate presence of Yahweh in the temple. When the temple was nevertheless rebuilt after the Babylonian exile, it was due to the desire by the returning priests to carry out the plans which the prophet Ezekiel had drawn up in Mesopotamia.

The views of those who had stayed behind in Jerusalem may also be gauged from the prophecies of Obadiah and from the Book of Lamentations. Obadiah launched bitter attacks on the Edomites,[1] who, according to Psalm 137, greatly enjoyed the fall of Jerusalem.[2] The Lamentations, which were written in an appropriately solemn meter—the *kinah*—and which, to this day, are recited annually in the synagogue on the ninth day of Ab in memory of the fall of Jerusalem and the destruction of the temple, attributed the national calamity to the sinfulness of the people of Judah. The loss of Jerusalem was considered God's just punishment; only true atonement and fervent prayers could restore the glory of the past. This book, which was later attributed to Jeremiah,

[1] Janssen: *op. cit.*, p. 108 f.
[2] Cf. Jer. 49 : 7–22; Ezek. 35; and Isa. 34. After the exile Edom had ceased to be an independent nation, and became part of an Arab federation under the leadership of Kedar.

expressed the mood of those who were left to see the ruins of their temple, and who witnessed the fulfilment of Jeremiah's gloomy prophecies.

Chronology of the Neo-Babylonian Empire

Nabopolasser (Nabu-apal-usur)	625–605
Nebuchadnezzar II (Nabu-kudurri-usur)	604–562
Evil-merodach (Awel-Marduk)	561–560
Neriglissar (Nergal-shar-usur)	559–556
Labashi-Marduk (Labashi-Marduk)	556
Nabonidus (Nabu-na'id)	555–538

XVI

RETURN AND RESTORATION

THE Persian Empire, which flourished from the reign of
Cyrus until its subjugation by Alexander the Great
(331 B.C.), was a vast region. Its kings ruled over the whole
of Palestine, subjected Egypt, and threatened the coasts of
Greece. Jerusalem became the capital of a Persian governor.
At first, the Persians simply adopted the Babylonian and
Assyrian system of provinces, giving Judah a new governor
but no independence. However, the change was significant,
for though the House of David was not restored, the Jews
had good reason to hope for better times. Accordingly, they
applied Isaiah's prophecies (44 : 28 and 45 : 1) to Cyrus,
and all Judah felt kindly towards a conqueror whose clear
desire it was to treat his many subjects with tolerance.

Naturally, Judah found it difficult to swallow the fact
that God's chosen people should owe their liberation not to
the House of David but to a foreigner. However, Isaiah
told them: "Woe to him who strives with his Maker, an
earthen vessel with the potter. Does the clay say to him
that fashions it, 'What are you making?'" (Isa. 45 : 9).

Despite the many disappointments, the authors of the
Book of Chronicles and Isaiah spoke of the return from
Babylonian captivity in terms reminiscent of the story of the
exodus from Egypt.

The restoration of the temple treasure and the building

of the new temple were entrusted to one Sheshbazzar, called the prince of Judah (Ezra 1 : 8, 11; 5 : 14, 16) who may well have been Shenazar, the grandson of King Jehoiakim (1 Chron. 3 : 18). The name was probably derived from the Babylonian Shamash-apal-usur, meaning "May Shamash preserve the son." According to Ezra 1 : 11, the treasures returned by him to Jerusalem consisted of 5,400 objects.

As far as we can tell, the Persian kings were disciples of Zoroaster and worshipped Ahura Mazda (Ormazd), the "Lord of Wisdom," much in the same way that the Jews worshipped Yahweh. Though both religions dispensed with images of their respective deities, the Jewish religion enjoyed no privileged status under Cyrus. The Persian king treated all his subject people as equals, not so much on religious principles as for reasons of political expediency.[1] While the Jews had great sympathy with Zoroastrianism, which had so much in common with their own religion, they nevertheless appreciated that there was an unbridgeable gulf between the dualism of the Persian religion and the monotheistic faith of Deut. 6 : 4. The belief in Yahweh's uniqueness was irreconcilable with the Persian view that Ormazd had to wage constant war against the god of darkness. An echo of this theological dispute can be found in Isa. 45 : 6–7, where we read: ". . . I am the Lord, and there is no other. I form the light and create darkness: I make weal and create woe. . . ."

Even so, many ideas stemming from the Zoroastrian religion have found their way into Judaism and thence into Christianity, mainly through such sects as the Essenes. Their religious outlook is known from the countless docu-

[1] H. H. Schaeder: *Das persische Weltreich* (*Vorträge der Friedrich Wilhelm Universitat Breslau*) 1940–1941, p. 21.

ments discovered since 1948 near the Dead Sea. Many of the tenets of the Essenes' faith—light *v.* darkness, heaven *v.* hell, the right path *v.* the wrong—have survived among us, and undoubtedly represent our spiritual heritage from the Persians. While there was no true syncretism, Persian religious ideas were most certainly discussed among the Jews and among Persia's other subject people.

At the beginning of the reign of Darius I (521–486 B.C.), there was a slim chance that the House of David might be restored to the throne of Judah. Herodotus reports that Darius' claim to the Persian crown was challenged by one Gaumata who claimed to be Smerdis the son of Cyrus and the brother of Cambyses, whom the latter had had done away with. Gaumata's pretensions shook the Persian Empire, and it is to him that the prophet Haggai must have been referring when he spoke of the overthrow of the Persian throne, which Judah would survive under the leadership of Zerubbabel[1] the son of Shealtiel. Zerubbabel, who is also mentioned by Zechariah, Ezra, and Nehemiah, brought a group of Jews back from Babylonian captivity.

At first he was merely charged with their repatriation, but soon afterwards the Persian emperor appointed him governor of Jerusalem. Zerubbabel was a grandson of the tragic King Jehoiachin—a descendant of David—and hence raised the illusion that the House of David had returned to the throne. However, we are told nothing about Zerubbabel's further history, and it seems likely that he became the willing or unwilling leader of a patriotic movement, and was deposed

[1] The Babylonian name was *Zer-babili* = "Scion of Babylon," but this is no proof that he was a Babylonian. E. Sellin (*Serubbabel, Ein Beitrag zur Geschichte der messianischen Erwartung und der Entstehung des Judentums*, Leipzig, 1898) has proposed that Zerubbabel was the suffering servant of Isa. 53, but this identification seems rather far-fetched.

by Darius as soon as the Persian King had re-established his own authority. In any case, the prophet Zechariah spoke out against Zerubbabel's revolutionary plans (Zech. 4 : 6).

Zerubbabel also played an important part in the High Priest Joshua's reconstruction of the temple. From the prophets Haggai and Zechariah, our informants about conditions in Jerusalem after the exile, we know that the original enthusiasm for the temple had quickly abated, and that the people felt bitterly disappointed. The harvest was too poor to feed the growing population; the value of money had fallen, and "he who earns wages earns wages to put them into a bag with holes" (Hag. 1 : 6). Haggai looked upon these visitations as signs of the Lord's anger that nothing at all had been done about building the new temple.

The protestations of Haggai and Zechariah were successful—on the 24th day of the 6th month of the 2nd year of the reign of Darius—in 520 B.C.—Zerubbabel and Joshua the High Priest ordered the new temple to be built. The work was completed four years later, thanks mainly to Persian subsidies, raised by local taxation. The new temple which was consecrated in 515 B.C. (Ezra. 6 : 15) was larger than Solomon's as we know from a visitor to Judea during the reign of Alexander the Great.[1] True, Ezra 3 : 12 tells us that many of the priests and Levites and chief of the fathers that had seen the first house (seventy years before) wept with a loud voice when the new foundation was laid, but their tears were merely rites of weeping (cf. Ps. 126 : 5–6), and not the expression of their sorrow about the smallness of the new temple. The main difference between the new and the old house was the absence of the Ark in the Holy of Holies. Instead, a rock—now covered by the famous Mosque

[1] Hecataeus of Abdera, quoted by Josephus in *Contra Apionem*, I, 22.

of Omar—projected from the ground, giving the temple the character of a natural shrine. The rock itself was looked upon as the cornerstone of the world. In addition, the distance between the congregation and the Holy of Holies had been greatly increased, reflecting the increasing distance between Yahweh and His people.

Haggai and Zechariah had placed high hopes in the new temple (Zech. 8 : 4–5), but they were soon disillusioned, for the people were laggard in contributing towards the upkeep of the Lord's House. Before the exile, the King had borne the costs, then for a time the Persians had helped out, now the people themselves were expected to pay for their religion with sacrificial offerings, and they responded by bringing inferior animals to the sacrifice (Mal. 1 : 8). An even greater threat to the continued existence of Judah was the hostility of the Samaritans who looked upon the new temple as the symbol of resurgence of their hated rivals in Jerusalem. Judah's chief protagonists in this struggle with Samaria were the prophets Ezra and Nehemiah.

We first meet Ezra as an official of the Persian King Artaxerxes I Longimanus (465–424). Ezra was a priest who could trace his lineage back to Aaron. His official title was "scribe of the law of the God of heaven" (Ezra 7 : 12). In other words, he was a kind of minister for Jewish affairs, in a state where the Jews, by number and influence, played an important part.

Ezra managed to persuade the Persians to give him a free hand in Jerusalem. As a scribe (*sopher*)[1] he had access to the

---

[1] H. H. Schaeder: *Esra der Schreiber (Beiträge zur historischem Theologie,* 5), Tübingen, 1930. Though the word *sāfĕrā* also meant "prophet" in the late Aramaic of the Targum, there is no reason to disagree with Schaeder that Ezra was a scribe first and foremost, who also acted as sage and prophet.

Persian archives in Susa containing the list of privileges granted to the Jews by Cyrus. Since these lists were written in Aramaic, the Book of Ezra included a number of passages in that language,[1] probably so that the Jews might quote the official laws concerning them in this exact wording.

Ezra's official orders were to go up with all those willing to accompany him to Jerusalem "to enquire concerning Judah and Jerusalem according to the law of thy God which is in thine hand" (Ezra 7 : 13–14). Armed with this authority, he led a large number of exiles back to Jerusalem. He was also offered a military escort which, however, he refused.

We do not know what law was in Ezra's hands; it seems unlikely that he had a written copy of all the laws of Moses. On his arrival in Jerusalem, Ezra was horrified to see how many mixed marriages had been contracted. Why he should have reacted so violently is incomprehensible, since both Abraham and Moses had taken alien wives with God's blessing. True, Deut. 7 : 1–4 stipulates that no Israelite should marry into any of the seven people of Canaan—for purely religious reasons—but these reasons did not apparently concern Ezra, for he made no effort to have the women converted. Instead, he advocated the racial purity of God's holy seed. Hence he may be called the founder of

---

[1] Cyrus' edict permitting the return to Judah (Ezra. 1 : 2–4) was translated by the Biblical author into Hebrew from the original Aramaic. The edict concerning the restoration of the temple is reported in the original (6 : 3–5) and so was the letter of the Samaritans to Artaxerxes (4 : 8–16), Artaxerxes' reply to the chancellor of Samaria (4 : 17–22), the letter of the governor of "Beyond the river" to Darius (5 : 8–17) and Artaxerxes' decree giving Ezra permission to take his people to Jerusalem (7 : 12–28).

Judaism. By the powers vested in him, he might easily have decreed the dissolution of all the offending marriages, but he preferred to persuade the people to take this step by themselves. His dramatic address to them is reported in Ezra 9. Whipping up the religious fervour of his compatriots, he made them swear a solemn oath of compliance. He then called an assembly of the people in Jerusalem "and all the people sat in the open square before the house of God, trembling because of this matter, and because of the heavy rain" (Ezra 10 : 9).

The Book of Ezra contains a list of the names of those who made use of the Persian King's permission to return to Jerusalem (Ezra 2 : 1–70);[1] a list of Ezra's travelling companions (8 : 1–20); and finally a list of all those who had contracted mixed marriages (10 : 18–44). Ezra must have compiled all these in order to keep the Persian King informed about his activities.

The Bible is silent about Ezra's subsequent fate, and extra-Biblical sources on the subject are conflicting. According to Josephus, Ezra was given a solemn state burial in Jerusalem,[2] while another tradition has it that he returned to Babylon where he was buried in a town bearing his name to this day.[3] The Talmud reports that Ezra was the first to introduce the square Hebrew script.[4] There is no

[1] This list is very similar to Neh. 7, but there are a number of differences between the two. According to H. L. Allrik, "The Lists of Zerubbabel (Neh. 7 and Ezr. 2) and the Hebrew Numerical Notation" (*BASOR*, 136, 1954, pp. 21–27), these differences are due to the Hebrew method of writing down numbers. Allrik argues that the two lists are copies of a census in which the figures were written down by means of strokes and not by letters.

[2] *Ant.*, XI, 5, 5.

[3] L. Ginzberg: *The Legends of the Jews*, Vol. IV, pp. 354–358.

[4] Cf., Ginzberg: *op. cit.*, Vol. VI, pp. 443 ff.

explicit mention of Ezra's failure to build an independent Jewish state with Jerusalem as its centre. However, his lack of success is apparent if we take it that the course of events was reported in chronological order by the author of the Book of Chronicles—who even added the books of Ezra and Nehemiah as the logical continuation to his own work. This order, though doubted by many critics, is consistent, for only by Ezra's political failure can Nehemiah's subsequent actions be reasonably explained. The Book of Nehemiah contains a series of memoirs probably written for the temple archives. According to the almost unanimous opinion of Biblical scholars, the whole book—with the exception of Chapters 8–10 and the two long lists (3 : 1–32 and 7 : 6–72)—is Nehemiah's personal account of his actions.

Nehemiah's way of life differed greatly from Ezra's. We meet him first as a cup-bearer at the court of King Artaxerxes I. While it was not unusual for a Jew to hold so high a position at the Persian court, it is surprising that Nehemiah agreed to taste the "unclean" wine of Gentiles with no apparent religious scruples. In the twentieth year of Artaxerxes' reign, Nehemiah was visited by his brother, who had been requested by a group of Jews to inform Nehemiah of the bad state of repair of Jerusalem's walls. The cup-bearer was then asked by his King why he had suddenly turned sad. When Nehemiah explained the cause of his sorrow, the King proved sympathetic, granted him special powers, and sent him to Jerusalem where, at first, he kept the purpose of his visit secret. After a few days, he rode out secretly in the night with only a few men, to inspect the state of the walls and the gutted gates. Much of our knowledge about the location of the gates of Jerusalem in the

fifth century is based on the account of this inspection.[1]
Only after he had taken stock of the situation did he reveal
his mission to the leading men: to bring about the rebuilding
of the walls. The leaders of the city all agreed with him at
once.

After the work had been started the enemies of Jerusalem
decided to act. Their leaders were Sanballat the Persian
governor of Samaria, Tobiah the Ammonite, and Geshem
the Arabian (Neh. 4 : 1 ff.).[2] These three men were the
spokesmen of all those who looked upon the reconstruction
of Jerusalem as a threat to their own safety. Because many
of their relatives had married into Jerusalem, they were
able to spread disaffection among the workers, who complained: "The strength of the bearers of burdens is fail-
ing, and there is much rubbish; we are not able to work
on the wall" (Neh. 4 : 10). When he discovered a plot
against him, Nehemiah was forced to arm his men (Neh.
4 : 17–18).

Social conditions in Jerusalem were far from ideal.
There were sharp class distinctions, and an increasing number
of idle desperadoes roamed the streets. In order to improve
matters, Nehemiah called upon the rich to write off all
debts. He himself, and his brother, set the example (Neh.
5 : 1 ff.).[2] Nehemiah also took steps to improve the lot of the
priests, the Levites, and of other temple servants.

[1] Cf. J. Simons: *Jerusalem in the O.T.*, Chapter VII (The City of
Nehemiah).

[2] Geshem's name appears on a silver bowl, discovered in the eastern
Nile delta. The inscription, in fifth-century Aramaic, states that the
bowl was an offering to the Arabian goddess Han-'ilat by "Cain, the
son of Geshem, King of Kedar." Cain had apparently assumed leadership over a number of Arabian tribes and also over Edom and Moab.
Cf. *BA*, 1955, p. 46 f.

After a stay of twelve years, Nehemiah returned to the court of King Artaxerxes. When he paid Jerusalem a second visit, he was sorely disappointed to see how little impact his words and actions had made. The high priest had married into the family of Tobiah the Ammonite, whom he had allowed to use a chamber in the temple as his office and store-room. Nehemiah had all Tobiah's belongings thrown into the street, and then ordered the chamber to be cleansed and again devoted to the use of the temple. By these and similar measures Nehemiah, like Ezra before him, ensured the purity of his people and prevented the Jews from disappearing in the Persian melting pot.

We must now return to the problem of the chronological order of the Books of Ezra and Nehemiah, which was posed anew when the Elephantine papyri, mentioned earlier, were acquired from Egypt in 1903–1911.[1] One group of these documents, formerly in the possession of an American collector and acquired by the Brooklyn Museum by bequest from his daughter, was only published in 1953.[2] From it we can reconstruct part of the history of the Jews in Elephantine.

The most important of all these papyri was one found by the Berlin Museum expedition: a letter by the Jews of Elephantine to Bagohi, the Persian governor of Judah. The letter, written in 407 B.C., complained that the High

[1] Two groups of these texts were re-published by A. Cowley: *Aramaic Papyri of the Fifth Century B.C.*, Oxford, 1923. New leather documents were published by G. R. Driver: *Aramaic Documents of the Fifth Century B.C.*, Oxford, 1957.

[2] E. G. Kraeling: *The Brooklyn Museum Aramaic Papyri*, New Haven, 1953. See also S. Segert: "Die neuen Editionen von Brooklyn Papyri und Arsam's Briefe in ihrer Bedeutung für die Bibelwissenschaft," *Archiv Orientálni*, 1956, pp. 383–403.

Priest Johanan had failed to reply to an earlier letter. Johanan was no doubt identical with the official by that name mentioned in Neh. 12 : 22 as the successor of Eliashib and Joiada, and as the predecessor of Jaddua. This is borne out by the fact that the document mentions that similar letters were sent out at the same time to Delaiah and Shelemiah, the sons of Sanballat, the Persian governor of Samaria. Now, we know from the Bible that Ezra went into the chamber of Johanan the son of Eliashib on the eve of the great assembly of the people. Since this event occurred in the seventh year of the reign of Artaxerxes (Ezra 7 : 7), Ezra must have arrived in Jerusalem in the year 457 B.C. (at least if the reference is to Artaxerxes I). According to Neh. 3 : 1, Nehemiah arrived in Jerusalem when Eliashib was High Priest, and in the twentieth year of the reign of Artaxerxes I Longimanus, i.e. in the year 444 B.C.

How then could Ezra have arrived in Jerusalem before Nehemiah, and yet have called on a high priest who only took office in Nehemiah's day? (Ezra 10 : 6–8). Scholars have tried to remove the contradiction by assuming that Ezra arrived in Jerusalem during the reign of Artaxerxes II Mnemon (404–358 B.C.), i.e. in 398 B.C. In that case the chronological order of the Bible must be reversed to explain the incidental reference to Johanan. The additional evidence that Ezra found Jerusalem surrounded by a wall (Ezra 9 : 9) is not conclusive, for first of all the Bible does not say, in so many words, that the wall had been repaired, and, in any case, the wall was attacked by the Samaritans just before Nehemiah arrived. All in all, we believe that the assumption that Nehemiah preceded Ezra, which was first propounded by A. van Hoonacker[1] and which has since gained much ground, does not agree with a picture based on *all* the known data.

With Nehemiah's diary ends the Biblical report of the fortunes of Jerusalem under the Persian Empire. With Jaddua, the last high priest to be mentioned (Neh. 12 : 22), a veil falls over the history of the city. The position of Jewry in the diaspora is somewhat better known through the Book of Esther and also through Chapters 3 and 6 of the Book of Daniel. The scene of the Book of Esther is the palace of the Persian king in Susa, which has been made vivid for us by the French excavations; its plot is Haman's attempt to destroy the Jews, and his downfall through Mordecai and Esther. There is much to be said for Hoschander's view[2] that the book was written against the historical background of the religious reforms of Artaxerxes II Mnemon. According to Berossos, a Babylonian priest who recorded the history of his people for the Seleucid ruler in the third century B.C., Artaxerxes II reintroduced idols into the Persian religion, and erected statues to Aphrodite-

[1] In a series of papers published between 1890 and 1924, particularly in "La succession chronologique Nèhémie—Esdras," *Revue Biblique*, 1923, pp. 481–494, and 1924, pp. 33–64. Among Hoonacker's leading supporters are H. H. Rowley: "The Chronological Order of Ezra and Nehemiah," *Ignaz Goldziher Memorial Volume*, Part I, Budapest 1948, pp. 117–149, with a most valuable bibliography. Reprinted in *The Servant of the Lord*, London, 1952, pp. 129–160. On Nehemiah see H. H. Rowley: "Nehemiah's Mission and its Background," *Bulletin of the John Rylands Library*, 37, 2, Manchester, 1955. Noth: *GI*, p. 288 f., holds that the question cannot be decided. For a novel view, maintaining the priority of Ezra, see J. Morgenstern: "The Dates of Ezra and Nehemiah," *JSS*, VII, 1962, pp. 1–12.

[2] J. Hoschander: *The Book of Esther in the Light of History*, Philadelphia, 1923.

Anahita in Babylon, Susa Ekbatana and other cities of his empire.

Only if participation in idolatry was, indeed, used as a token of loyalty to the Persian king, does Dan. 3 make real sense. The Bible records the King's proclamation (Dan. 3 : 4 ff.) in Aramaic, thus reflecting the atmosphere of Persian times.[1] The name of Nebuchadnezzar is used as a synonym for "idol-worshipping tyrant."[2] Actually it is the King of Persia who is meant. Dan. 3 is clearly a call to the faithful to abide by the law of Moses and to strengthen them against the fear of martyrdom. True, Daniel was rescued from the lions' den by the King himself (Dan. 6), but the story of the three youths in the fiery furnace and the story of Haman show clearly what may happen if tyrants side with the enemies of the Jewish people. A rebirth of the ancient Persian religion—possibly as a means of staying the decay of the empire—may well have been the chief cause of violent anti-Jewish excesses. The differences between Jews and Gentiles which had tended to disappear under the Achaemenians, had once again become more marked, for the Jews alone refused to bow down before idols. For the Hellenistic era this situation became aggravated. Jewish

---

[1] H. H. Schaeder: *Iranische Beiträge, I* (*Schriften der Königsberger Gelehrten Gesellschaft, Geisteswissenscheftliche Klasse*, 6 Jahr, Heft 5) Halle, 1930, examines this use of Aramaic in the Bible.

[2] This fact is confirmed by one of the texts discovered near Qumran, containing an Aramaic prayer of Nabonidus as part of a cycle of Daniel stories, in which Nabonidus is called a King of Assyria. The text was published by J. T. Milik as "Prière de Nabonide et autres écrits d'un cycle de Daniel," *Revue Biblique*, 1956, pp. 407–415. L. Woolley: *Ur of the Chaldees*, London, 1950, pp. 151–52, suggests that Nebuchadnezzar's rebuilding of the temple in Ur may explain Dan. 3. But this rests on very slender foundations.

stubbornness led to anti-Jewish riots, particularly in Alexandria, where every festival, every game, and every contest was associated with the gods. No wonder then that the Greek translation of the Book of Esther was later provided with various addenda the main purpose of which was to stress the perilous position of the Jews amidst their Greek and Egyptian hosts.

XVII

THE SELEUCID EMPIRE

WE know very little more about the history of Jerusalem during the decline of the Persian Empire, or about the events following Ezra and Nehemiah's successful attempts to obtain a measure of autonomy for Judah, than that Jerusalem had become the centre of a small Jewish state, governed by a high priest. Josephus' brief accounts covering the period between Nehemiah and the rise of Alexander the Great indicate that the Jews had largely succeeded in preserving their national identity, particularly from the Samaritans. However, there was strong opposition—even from the priesthood—to the law forbidding intermarriages. We also know that, because of a murder in the temple, the Persian government imposed a fine of fifty drachmas for every lamb offered during the daily sacrifice.

There is no reason to believe that Alexander's victory at Issus (333 B.C.) affected the status of Jerusalem in any basic way. All that happened was that the overlord changed his name—taxes and soldiers had now to be supplied to the Greeks instead of to the Persians. Hence the silence of Jewish sources about the momentous historical events that shook the Near East at the time. True, the author of the Book of Daniel called Alexander "the he-goat who came from the West on the face of the whole earth, and touched not the ground" (Dan. 8 : 5), and who later smote the ram with two horns, but the mere fact that the Books of Daniel, Maccabees and Josephus mention Alexander's campaigns only by the way, is clear evidence that, at first, Greek rule did not affect the Jews.[1] Josephus' detailed description of the meeting outside Jerusalem between Alexander and the High Priest is based on later Jewish "Alexander-legends," all built round a supposed promise of the conqueror to allow the Jews to live according to the laws of their fathers (Josephus: *Ant.*, XI, 8, 4–5). It seems probable that, after the capture of Gaza in 332 B.C., Alexander visited Jerusalem where he offered sacrifices to the God of the Jews, much as he later sacrificed to the gods of Egypt.

The Persian Empire had made way for the Greek Empire. Now, Greek culture had not been completely unknown in Asia, even before the advent of Alexander. As early as the seventh century B.C., Greek merchants had travelled through Egypt and Western Asia, spreading Greek ideas and products wherever they went. The Persian kings held the work of Greek craftsmen and artists in such high regard that, in about 500 B.C., they called them in to help embellish the palace at Susa. We know that, in the fifth century B.C., Herodotus and Xenophon made adventurous journeys to Western Asia, and we may take it that they helped to spread Greek culture wherever they went. Thus Greek words and concepts found their way into the official Aramaic, which, under King Darius I, was the *lingua franca* of the Persian Empire. No wonder then that such words as *kitharis* (zither) and *psalterion* in Dan. 3, crop up precisely in a report dealing with the position of the Jews in the Persian

---

[1] It is improbable that Zech. 9: 1–8 is an allusion to Alexander the Great (M. Delcor: "Les allusions à Alexandre le Grand dans Zach. IX 1–8," *VT*, 1951, pp. 110 ff.).

Empire. It was the "people of Javan" to whom the coastal peoples of Palestine sold Jewish slaves (Joel 3 : 6) long before Alexander the Great came to power. Occasional archaeological finds emphasise this cultural influence more strongly than even the most colourful accounts of the Maccabean War. We know today that Greek coins were being copied by Persian satraps in the fourth century B.C., and that Judah too was given permission to mint her own silver coins, depicting Attic temples and inscribed with the provincial name Jehud = Judah. Hence, by the time Alexander came on the scene, the peaceful Hellenisation of Judah was well under way—his victories merely accelerated the process. When, after Alexander's death (323 B.C.) and after the resulting chaos, order had once again been restored, and the provinces of the various *diadochi* or "successors" of Alexander were clearly defined, Jerusalem became part of the Ptolemaic realm, governed from Egypt. With short interruptions Ptolemaic rule lasted for the whole of the third century B.C. We know much more about the conditions of the Jews in the Egyptian diaspora at the time than about events in Jerusalem. This is mainly due to the fact that papyri keep particularly well in the dry climate of Egypt. From hints in these documents we can, however, make a number of deductions about developments in Palestine itself, which for more than a century was the bone of contention between the Ptolemaic and the Seleucid Empires. As the battlefield of the mightiest of the *diadochi*, Judah had become an inhospitable region, and thousands of its inhabitants migrated to the towns founded by Ptolemy, particularly to Alexandria in the Nile delta, which granted all foreigners full citizenship.

Life in Judah became more peaceful when a Seleucid

king, Antiochus III, finally conquered Jerusalem in 200 B.C., and granted the town a number of privileges in an edict recorded by Josephus, and originally incorporated in a letter to Ptolemy, the reigning High Priest and commander of Coele-Syria and Phoenicia, who had gone over to Antiochus III from the Egyptian camp. Since Josephus' rendering of the edict is now generally held to be correct in substance, the letter to Ptolemy is the key to our understanding of the subsequent events which reached their climax in the Maccabean Wars. The letter is worth quoting:

"King Antiochus to Ptolemy, greetings. Whereas, immediately upon entering their country we were promised loyalty by the Jews whose Council of Elders received us solemnly upon our entering their city, providing all necessities for our army and our elephants, and giving us active support in capturing the Egyptian garrison in the Acra, we have decreed, in accordance with our religious belief, to grant a contribution to their temple sacrifices, to wit sacrificial animals, wine, oil, myrrh up to 20,000 pieces of silver, fine flour for baking into shewbread according to their law, in all 1,460 measures of wheat and 375 measures of salt. It is our wish that all these things be rendered unto them according to our edict. Further we have decided to carry out the restoration of their temple, their hall of pillars, and of everything else belonging thereto. Moreover, any belonging to this people may live unmolested in accordance with their laws. Elders, priests, temple scribes and cantors are exempted from the head tax, the royal tax, and the salt tax. So that the population of Jerusalem may grow more speedily, we exempt all citizens together with all those returning before the month of Hyperbeteos, from paying taxes for three years. Finally, we restore full freedom to all those who have been carried off as slaves from the city, and order that their property be returned to them." (*Ant.*, XII, 3, 3.)

As Palestine was part of the Seleucid Empire from *c.* 200 B.C. we must now look more closely at the structure and institutions of this commonwealth of nations.

Though the name "Seleucid Empire" was coined by seventeenth-century European historians, the ancients themselves realised that the advent of Seleucus I in 312 B.C. ushered in a new era, and began a new calendar accordingly. This era was used in the first book of the Maccabees though, unlike the Greeks, whose year began in the Autumn, the Jews of that time began their year in the Spring. Hence for the Jews, the Seleucid era begins on the 1st Nisan 311 B.C. Unfortunately the first book of Maccabees often confuses the Jewish and the official years, while the second book usually adheres to the Greek year. As a result, the Maccabean chronology poses a host of special problems.

Unlike the Ptolemaic Empire, the so-called Seleucid Empire was far too vast to be completely unified. It included peoples of all kinds. It stretched from the coasts of Asia Minor and Palestine as far as the Indus, and bordered on the Caspian Sea and the Persian Gulf. Its kings, despite their Greek descent, were expected to behave like Oriental potentates and to give proof of their prowess in the field. Hence they constantly waged wars, and hence so many of them were killed. In fact, between 312 and 129, only two Seleucids died a natural death. Of the rest, two were murdered in their youth, and all the others fell in the field. Kings commanding their own army were the embodiment of political power, and laws unto themselves. Thus Seleucus I justified an unpopular step based on the principle that the King could do no wrong.

No wonder that there was no popular representation under the Seleucids—not even a Council of Elders.[1] Instead there was an oligarchy consisting of the *philoi*—"friends," i.e. loyal adherents—whom the King chose as he liked, and whose counsel he might seek during crises. Antiochus Epiphanus' reply to a request by the Samaritans contained the phrase: "During a meeting with our friends . . ." (Josephus, *Ant.*, XII, 5, 5). From I Maccabees we know something of how the friends were distinguished by rank and position. Alexander Balas appointed Jonathan "friend" and High Priest of Jerusalem. As High Priest he was clothed in purple, wore a golden crown, and was called "Brother" by the King. Two years later, Jonathan was appointed *protos philos* (first among the friends), and after another three years he was presented with a golden buckle, "usually given to such as are of the king's blood." Later, when Jonathan deserted Alexander Balas and went over to Demetrius II and Antiochus VI, these titles and honours had to be granted anew. Hence, when Antiochus VI invited Jonathan to drink from a golden bowl, to clothe himself in purple and to wear his golden buckle, he indicated that he, too, looked upon Jonathan as "first friend" (cf. I Macc. 10 and 11).

Naturally, an autocracy of that type could only maintain itself in power with the help of a large and mobile army. Thus, we know that Seleucus I was able to throw more than 20,000 foot soldiers, 12,000 horsemen, 100 chariots, and 480

[1] E. Bickermann: *Institutions des Séleucides*, Paris, 1938. The author emphasises the historical continuity between Persian and Roman rule over the Near East.

elephants into one of his famous battles; that 62,000 foot soldiers and 6,000 horsemen were deployed at the Battle of Raphia (217 B.C.) and that Antiochus VII fought the Persians with an army of 80,000 men. The army was made up of one part mercenaries and one part conscripts from among the subject nations, each of whom had to supply a quota of able-bodied men.

The Seleucid treasury was continuously being depleted by warfare, particularly when the Romans began to gain the upper hand. To meet the rising expenses a series of levies was introduced, among which the communal tax, the *phoros*, was the most important. The *phoros* had been imposed since the time of Darius I. The Roman Emperors later eased the burden by varying the levy according to the result of the harvest, but the Seleucids simply fixed the amount according to their needs. They also appointed High Priests by "tender," selecting such who undertook to bring in the largest amount. By this means, the suzerain was able to increase the levy on Jerusalem from 300 to 360 and finally to 390 talents. In relating how Demetrius II was forced to grant Jerusalem exemption from the *phoros* by the High Priest Simon, the author of First Maccabees declares that "the yoke of the heathen was taken away from Israel" (1 Macc. 13 : 41)—a proof that the Jews considered the tax a sign of bondage. It must, however, be remembered that the Seleucids left the collection of taxes in the hands of local officials, e.g. of the High Priest in Jerusalem, and never collected directly.

In addition to the *phoros*, other taxes were imposed as well, but we know only about the tax arrangements in Jerusalem, where Antiochus III collected head money, crown taxes, salt taxes and indirect taxes, apart from the *phoros*. Only the members of the Sanhedrin and the priests were exempt from direct taxes and King Antiochus III even bore the costs of the upkeep of the temple. By the time Jonathan became High Priest (152 B.C.), things had changed for the worse: a very high land tax and a "purchase tax" of ten per cent were added, and even the priests' income was taxed, though the King continued to contribute towards the upkeep of the temple and of the Jewish cult. Later, the High Priest John Hyrcanus had to agree to submit a further 500 talents, but the defeat of Antiochus VII by the Parthians (129 B.C.) absolved him of this obligation. If the King needed more money still, he would not shrink from laying his hands on even temple treasures. Thus Antiochus III was killed while robbing a shrine, and Antiochus IV while trying to plunder the temple of Artemis in Elam.

Within the far-flung Seleucid Empire were found a number of Greek colonies organised on the Hellenistic pattern. However, by the side of the Greek *polis* (city), there existed other social structures called *ethnos* (people) and *dynastes* (ruler), respectively. According to Strabo, four *ethne* existed in Syria, Coele-Syria, and Phoenicia, though the only one about which we know anything at all is the Jewish *ethnos*. The King, if he so wished, could grant every city a special status, of which the *lex provincae* or provincial law of the Romans was merely an adaptation. Hence, from the time of the Persian Empire onwards, Jerusalem was governed by a High Priest and by the Sanhedrin, and not even the Seleucids changed its status, except during the three years of the Maccabean rebellion.

We must now return to the letter of Antiochus III to Ptolemy of which we spoke earlier. The most important sentences in it read:

"Moreover, any belonging to this people may live unmolested in accordance with their laws. Elders, priests, temple scribes, and cantors are exempted from the head tax, the royal tax, and the salt tax."

Clearly, the priesthood in this temple state enjoyed special privileges, and Jerusalem was granted the right to live according to its own religious customs, as was the rest of the Jewish population. Thus the Seleucid King pledged his powers to preserve the Sabbath, to ban the import of impure animals, and to bar the Holy of Holies to all strangers. As every reader of the New Testament knows, this state of affairs was preserved even under the Romans. Oddly enough, the Sovereign reserved the right to replace the High Priest who, to him, was no more than his deputy in Jerusalem charged with collecting taxes, and raising a militia, and who also acted as a link between the Jewish people and their neighbours. The priestly rulers of the *ethnos* of Jerusalem enjoyed so great a measure of independence that a conflict could only arise if a Seleucid king decided to meddle in matters on which all the Jews were united. This is precisely what happened under Antiochus IV Epiphanes, and led to the Maccabean revolt.

To this day, our knowledge of the history of Palestine after Alexander the Great is chiefly based on only two sources: the two books of the Maccabees and the works of Flavius Josephus. Greek and Roman historians paid little attention to the Jewish people—hence what few comments they did make about the Jews have unusual historical importance.[1] The Talmud and the Midrashim have also preserved a record of ancient traditions from which later

[1] Conveniently collected in text and translation by Th. Reinach: *Textes d'anteurs grecs et romains au Judaisme*, Paris, 1895.

historians have been able to trace the spiritual development of Judaism,[1] and the recent surprising discovery of scrolls and fragments of texts near Qumran on the Dead Sea has thrown much light on the same development and hence on the origins of Christianity.[2] For the history of the Jews after A.D. 70 our most important post-classical sources are Dio Cassius, who wrote a history in A.D. 210–220. Extant fragments of this Greek work are the main sources of our knowledge of Bar Cochba's struggle against the Emperor Hadrian (A.D. 132–135).

Maccabees 1 and 2, and the most important works of Josephus (*History of the Jewish War; Jewish Antiquities*), have come to be looked upon as biased writings. Above all the "documents" on which Josephus based his account are now generally considered to be of different origin from those used in Maccabees 1 and 2, though not thereby becoming less reliable or less important. It is precisely by analysing these documents that Bickermann has arrived at a new and surprising view of the Maccabean rebellion.[3] From an investigation of Greek papyri we know that the formal language used in the Books of the Maccabees is authentic, and also how to arrange the material in an order that was previously considered impossible.

1 Maccabees is a Greek work translated from the Hebrew.[4]

---

[1] See G. F. Moore: *Judaism*, Vol. I, Cambridge, 1927, and the Hebrew work by Y. F. Boer (*Israel among the Nations*) published in Jerusalem in 1955.

[2] J. M. Allegro: *The Dead Sea Scrolls*, London, 1956.

[3] E. Bickermann: *Der Gott der Makkabäer*, Berlin, 1937.

[4] For commentaries on the Books of the Maccabees, cf. F. M. Abel: *Les livres des Maccabées*, Paris, 1949. For the text, translation and commentary cf. S. S. Tedesche and S. Zeitlin: *Jewish Apocryphal Literature* (N.Y., 1950 and 1954).

It deals with the history of the Jews in Palestine from 175 to 135 B.C., and is a typical example of dynastic history. The book was written for the express purpose of glorifying the Maccabean rulers, probably in the time of John Hyrcanus, who became High Priest in 134 B.C. The author was so much an admirer of his Maccabean heroes, that he simply identified them and their followers with the people of Israel, though many orthodox Jews preferred the Greek way of life, and others, whose Jewishness was purely religious, looked upon the martial pomp of the Maccabeans with disfavour. Both groups were dismissed as enemies of Israel by the author of 1 Maccabees, who drew everything in black and white: Israel and the Maccabees were the heroes, and their enemies the villains. Many of his sayings were taken from the Old Testament, for instance the frequently recurring phrase: "The land had rest" (cf. Joshua. 11 : 23; 1 Macc. 7 : 50, 9 : 57, 14 : 4).

While 1 Maccabees begins with the reign of Alexander the Great and then goes on to describe the misdeeds of the Seleucids, 2 Maccabees has another, quite characteristic, beginning: a festive epistle from the priesthood in Jerusalem to the Jews in Egypt and a preface (2 Macc. 2 : 19–32) mentioning Jason of Cyrene. Jason was an Egyptian Jew who had written a history in five books on which the author of 2 Maccabees based his own work. Since the beginnings of Maccabees 1 and 2 agree in certain respects, we may take it that Jason also inspired 1 Maccabees. After this introduction, 2 Maccabees immediately tackles what, for the author, was the most important subject: Heliodorus' attempted robbery of the temple treasure and his ensuing punishment. For the author, the wheel of Israel's history was spun by a power other than that of the heathen. Israel's own sin was the main cause of her downfall. Even so, 2 Maccabees is more strongly influenced by Greek ideas than 1 Maccabees.

From Jason of Cyrene, the author of 2 Maccabees learned of, and repeated, a non-Jewish tradition according to which Antiochus IV attacked the Jews because of their rebelliousness. Then as now, propaganda was a great and lying weapon, and while the Seleucids emphasised the brigandage of the Jews, the latter called the Seleucids temple-robbers. Later still, classical authors chose to represent King Antiochus' fight against the Jews as a struggle between a civilised and a barbarous people. This view is expressed chiefly by Tacitus[1] and also by the distorted account of Diodorus quoting Poseidonios. Diodorus repeated the following fable:

> "Antiochus, also named Epiphanes, who defeated the Jews in war, proceeded to the shrine which, according to custom, only the high priest was permitted to enter. Here he found a graven image of a man with a flowing beard who, bearing a book in his hand, was sitting on an ass. He thought that the image was of Moses, the founder of Jerusalem, who had gathered his people into a nation and who had forced their strange and inhuman customs upon them."

The rest of the report is in much the same vein—a strange fusion of Seleucid and Jewish propaganda.

2 Maccabees is greatly revered by Catholic Christianity, which looks upon the deeds of Heliodorus and his punishment as symbols of the divine punishment of all the enemies of the church. Again, 2 Maccabees 6 and 7 describe acts of martyrdom, which are rightly considered as Christian

[1] Hist. V, 2–13.

examples, imbued as they are with Hellenistic rather than with Jewish pathos.

We owe the preservation of Josephus' works much more to the Christians than to the Jews. The church has always considered Josephus one of the few non-Christian witnesses of the historicity of Christ's life on earth. The relevant passage is found in *Ant.* XVIII, 3, 3, and is so obviously a later addition, that it is generally considered apocryphal. However, it may very well have been added by Josephus himself in order to curry favour with the Christians. In that case, the passage tells us what the Christians among whom Josephus moved liked to have a non-Christian say about Jesus. This view fits in well with what we know of Josephus the historian.

Scholars have often pointed to the discrepancies between Josephus' *Jewish War* and his *Antiquities*, although much in the former is a repetition of the latter. These discrepancies are generally ascribed to the split personality of Josephus, but this view ignores the fact that Josephus had different motives in writing the two works. One can only grasp the spirit of the *Jewish War* if one bears in mind the impact on Josephus of Vespasian's capture of Jotopata, the Galilean fortress.[1] There is no reason to doubt the truth of the essential facts reported by him. When he was brought before Vespasian from the cave in which he had hidden himself, Josephus saved his life by predicting that Vespasian would become emperor and bring peace. Once this prophecy was fulfilled, Josephus' chains would be broken as a sign of his innocence. The two reports (*Jewish War*, III 8, 9, and *Ant.* IV, 10, 7) are the centre of the whole story. They show us Josephus as a Jew steeped in the traditions of his

[1] Cf. W. Weber: *Josephus und Vespasian*, Leipzig, 1921.

people, and greeting the foreign ruler as a Messiah, much as the Persian King Cyrus had been welcomed in former days (Isa. 44 : 28 and 45 : 1).

This Messianic hope was kindled in Josephus not only by his personal meeting with Vespasian, but also by his gratitude to the man who had saved his life. It was not treason that caused him to plead with the people of Jerusalem to surrender to Vespasian and Titus. Josephus never denied his faith, but he was convinced that Vespasian alone could save the Jews. Hence his book ends appropriately (apart from a few additional reports of minor importance) with the building of a Temple of Peace (*Jewish War*, VII, 5, 7). Josephus, too, was a dynastic historian, and probably consulted the *commentarii*—the reports of eyewitnesses—for he describes events which he could not possibly have seen himself, and wove them into a history glorifying the imperial house of Flavius, a name which Josephus himself adopted.

The *Antiquities* reflect an entirely different spirit. They were written in order to arouse sympathy for the Jewish people. Unlike the *Jewish War*, they contain no authentic reports about decisive events, but consist of a host of documents and quotations stressing the dignity and importance of Judaism. One of Josephus' main sources was Nicolaus of Damascus, the secretary of Herod the Great, and the latter's undiscriminating biographer. Josephus drew from Nicolaus' work the many details about Herod and his house which only an initiate could know. Josephus also quoted Strabo in support of the Jews, and combed the archives for any other documents that might serve his purpose (*Ant.* XIV, 10). Luckily, Josephus did not simply condense these documents into a concise history, but quoted them in full.

Thus Josephus became the defender of a people who rejected him, because they could not follow his thoughts. From his *Autobiography* we know that his Jewish compatriots repeatedly complained of him to the Flavian emperors, and that they had some measure of success with Domitian, the last of the line. At that time, Josephus made contact with the Roman publisher Epaphroditus who was issuing books on current events. Perhaps people of our generation—who remember Hitler's murders of the Jews and also the creation of the State of Israel—will understand the interest with which the Romans, having the Arch of Titus constantly before their eyes, followed the fortunes of the Jewish people.[1] This interest of his Roman readers was fully met by Josephus, who had finally broken with the dynasty of the Flavians, and who now enjoyed the protection of a rich Roman publisher. The break with the Flavians also explains why Josephus judged Herod Agrippa I and II so harshly. A literary dispute was unleashed when one Justus from Tiberius directed a spirited attack on Josephus' historical views. Justus represented the Jewish view that the Septuagint was no true translation of the original Hebrew, and accused Josephus of misrepresenting the Holy Scriptures. It has been suggested that Josephus, then an old man, adopted Christian views in order to curry favour with the growing Christian movement, and that he allowed a Christian to dictate *Ant.*, XVIII, 3, 3 to him.[2] This claim is quite unsubstantiated, though, as we have said, it was the church rather than the synagogue which kept the memory of Josephus alive.

[1] F. M. Th. de Liagre Böhl: *Die Juden im Urteil der griechischen und römischen Schriftsteller*, Groningen, 1953, pp. 126 ff. The keeping of the Sabbath, circumcision and abstention from pork were especially noted.

[2] R. Laqueur: *Der Jüdische Historiker Flavius Josephus*, Giessen, 1920.

With some reservations, we must mention yet another historical source: the apocalyptic books. While this type of literature, examples of which are found in Dan. 8–12, and the Book of Enoch, is admittedly not history in the customary sense, it has done more to clarify Jewish history than all the authors who have concentrated on factual events alone. Apocalyptic literature represents a grandiose attempt to discover the hidden meaning of history, as a means of predicting the future. With mighty sweeps of the pen, the apocalyptic writers tried to write Israel's history in universal terms.

The apocalyptic writers did not leave their successors with any rules for interpreting their sayings. In all probability they were secret or open opponents of the ruling power, and only escaped the watchful eye of the censorship by using a secret code of their own. Though their symbolic allusions were meant to apply to all times, they were all based on actual events of great importance, and hence are invaluable historical sources. Such an event, for instance, was the famine during the Maccabean uprising against Antiochus Epiphanes. The apocalyptic writers represented the views of the extremest orthodoxy. Their faith in God and His law was such that they refused to obey any temporal ruler. They invariably wondered when God would save His people, or, in a more pessimistic mood, when God would impose His just punishment.

In their calculations, long historical periods were generally condensed into brief spans of time. Even so, the apocalyptic texts provide us with important historical material, particularly when the events they describe occurred in the time of the writers themselves (e.g. Dan. 11 : 21–39, describing the reign of Antiochus Epiphanes). Moreover, their view that history repeats itself has had important effects on western historiography from St. Augustine onwards. It strikes us that the apocalyptics made, rather than wrote, history. Among the Dead Sea scrolls discovered in 1947, and written by the Essenes or a related sect, there was one with the title, "The War between the Sons of Light and the Sons of Darkness." If this scroll was written in the second century B.C., as we have reason to believe, it reflects the kind of thought that was put into practice in the Maccabean uprising. These strict apocalypticists paved the way for a great struggle against the forces of evil, which, to them, was not concluded with the victory of Judas Maccabaeus.

From the apocalyptic writers we learn that spiritual history cannot be separated from political history. This is true of all peoples, but particularly of Israel in whose history few battles were fought that lacked a spiritual motive. Each party or sect in Israel contributed towards the moulding of the nation, and kings as well as high priests were exponents of spiritual trends.[1]

[1] The standard work on Jewish history of New Testament times E. Schürer: *Geschichte des jüdischen Volkes im Zeitalter Jesu Christi*, 4th edition, Leipzig, 1901–1909. More recent material is included in F. M. Abel: *Histoire de la Palestine depuis la conquête d'Alexandre jusqu'à l'invasion Arabe*, Vols. I and II (pp. 1–104), Paris, 1952. See also R. H. Pfeiffer: *History of New Testament Times with an Introduction to the Apocrypha*, N.Y., 1949. Archaeological discoveries are daily increasing our store of knowledge, and demand certain revisions of our views. The archaeological material known before 1934 is found in C. Watzinger: *Denkmäler Palestina's*, Vol. II, Leipzig, 1935. Data relating to the territory of Israel are discussed in great detail in M. Avi Yonah and S. Yeivin's Hebrew work: *The Antiquities of Israel*, Tel Aviv, 1955.

XVIII

THE MACCABEAN WAR

SOON after Antiochus IV Epiphanes became Seleucid ruler in the winter of 176–175 B.C., he dismissed Onias, the High Priest, and appointed Onias' brother Jesus, better known as Jason, in his stead. This step was but one of many taken to withdraw the privileges granted the Jews by Antiochus III. 2 Maccabees blames all the dire consequences on Jason and his successors. Thus we are told that Jason set up a gymnasium and a playing field for training the youth and that the gymnasts were granted special privileges by the King (2 Macc. 4: 9). Now the building of a gymnasium ran counter to Jewish custom, for this purely Greek institution involved public displays of nudity. And yet such indecency was being encouraged by the High Priest himself!

Pious Jews were outraged even further when Jason was replaced by Menelaus, who not only imposed still heavier taxes but, as the willing tool of Antiochus IV, acquiesced when the King carried off the entire temple treasure in 169 B.C. Previously, Seleucus IV had made a similar attempt with the help of his minister Heliodorus. At that time, the priests disguised as angels on horseback, had frightened the heathen off. Afterwards the pious fraud of the priests was reported to the King by one Simon, the market supervisor, who felt his livelihood threatened by the ban on the import of impure goods into the Holy City. Only because of the sudden death of Seleucus IV was no punitive expedition sent against Jerusalem. In other words, Antiochus IV merely continued his predecessor's policies.

From 2 Maccabees and allusions in such apocalyptic writings as Enoch we may infer that Menelaus had a hand in the murder of the High Priest Onias (cf. 2 Macc. 4: 33–38 and Enoch 90: 8). Other data suggest that Onias fled to Egypt where he founded the temple of Leontopolis, closed in A.D. 73 on the orders of Vespasian. In either case, soon after his dismissal, Jason organised a party of Onias supporters to fight the Seleucids. It would be wrong, however, to make too much of a conflict between two Jewish clerical parties, one supported by Egypt and the other by Syria, or to consider Jason a defender of Judaism against the Hellenistic ideals of Menelaus and his adherents. The fact was simply that internal pressure drove the party of Onias in a different direction.

When Antiochus Epiphanes, the successor of Seleucus IV, was defeated during a campaign against Egypt, the Ptolemaic party took courage and conquered Jerusalem under Jason's leadership. Antiochus sent a punitive expedition against them and, in 168 B.C., he built the Acra, a citadel facing the Temple Hill. The walls of Jerusalem were pulled down, and the Acra was turned into a Seleucid stronghold and hence a place of refuge for the adherents of Menelaus. It was also made a Greek *polis* and, as such, set over the *ethnos* of Jerusalem. Jewish institutions were further threatened when the nameless Jewish God—or the "Lord of Heaven," as Israel's masters had called Him ever since the Achemenids—was given the official name of Zeus Olympios by the Greeks, who—as we know from Herodotus—looked upon divine anonymity as a sign of barbarism. A second altar was erected on top of the existing one in the temple, which the Book of Daniel calls *shikkuts shomem* (abomination of desolation) as a pun on *ba'al shamayim* (Lord of Heaven) (Dan. 12: 11; cf. Dan. 9: 27 and 11: 31).[1]

Minor differences aside, however, the cult of the Lord of Heaven remained unchanged. For instance, the temple was not rebuilt, as it would have been had the Hellenisation of the Jewish religion been carried out consistently. The design of Semitic temples with their inaccessible shrines and their gradual transition from profane to sacred areas, differed radically from that of Greek temples with their *cellae* and idols, open to all worshippers. The *Seleucid* commander Nicanor threatened to destroy the temple and the altar and to erect "a notable temple unto Bacchus" unless Judas Maccabeus was delivered to him (2 Macc. 14: 31–33). However, he failed to put this threat into practice. According to Jerome (quoting Porphyry) an image of Zeus was erected in the temple of Jerusalem, but since Jewish sources are silent about what would have been a terrible outrage, we may take it that this report is inaccurate.

On the other hand, certain rites of Israel's despised neighbours were introduced into the worship of the Lord of Heaven. E. Bickermann, to whom we owe an original and profound study of the motives of the Maccabean rebellion,[2] has rightly suggested that the "abomination of desolation" was no more than a stone representing a godhead, thus degrading the altar into a mere plinth for such deities as Jupiter Lapis.

[1] H. H. Rowley: "Menelaus and the Abomination of Desolation," in *Studia Orientalia Joanni Pedersen dedicata*, 1953, pp. 303–315, suggests, on the basis of 1 Macc. 1: 54, that an image was set upon the real altar, and that a heathen altar was placed facing the image.

[2] E. Bickermann: *Der Gott der Makkabäer*, Berlin, 1937, p. 109.

This degradation robbed the divine service of its exclusive character. The popular idolatry of old, which had never died out, came into its own once again, and a host of new altars was erected all over the country. Oddly enough, this urge to abandon the ancestral religion coincided with renewed religious persecutions of the Jews. Though temple desecrations and changes of religion were frequent in antiquity, we have to go back to the time of the Pharaoh Ikhnaton to find a similar attempt at compulsory conversion. What is stranger still is that the persecution of the orthodox was restricted to the area of the former *ethnos* of Jerusalem. Josephus has recorded a petition by the inhabitants of Samaria to Antiochus IV and the King's reply. The Samaritans complained that they were looked upon as Jews and held responsible for Jewish crimes. They pleaded for protection against this calumny, and the King granted their request (*Ant.*, XII, 5, 5). Josephus' version of the original petition and of the King's reply to Nicanor reflect the diplomatic style of contemporary papyri, and must therefore be considered authentic and of great historical importance. They show that the Samaritans, as self-confessed lovers of all things Greek, were allowed to keep the Sabbath, to circumcise their sons, and to observe all the other religious laws, while orthodox Jews in nearby Jerusalem were being burned alive in scrolls of the law for doing just these things.

Hence it would appear that Bickermann is correct to challenge the common view that Antiochus intended to Hellenise all his subjects. This view was also held by those classical writers who, for anti-Semitic reasons, fêted Antiochus Epiphanes as the King who had brought culture to a barbaric and obstinate people. In fact, Antiochus was anything but a passionate proselytiser, for we know that he did nothing to stop the worshipping of the goddess Nanaia in Susa, of the six-winged god in Byblos, or of Marduk in Babylon. Antiochus simply sided with Menelaus whom he had lawfully appointed High Priest, and who, according to Josephus, was a bad and godless man. It was for sheer love of power that Menelaus forced the people to sin against the laws of the Fathers (*Ant.*, XII, 9, 7).

Menelaus was the leader of those "that forsake the holy covenant" (Dan. 11:30), and who wanted to end the strict segregation of the Jews enforced by Ezra and Nehemiah. Previously, Jewish segregation had been guaranteed by the heathen overlords, but from 168 B.C. onwards, the state started to press for assimilation. In fact, to the Greeks, Menelaus' opponents were simply a band of rebels. However Menelaus was not as bad as he has been painted, for, by depriving the Jews of their special privileges, he really hoped to abolish the special taxes imposed on them. The First Book of Maccabees tells us that many Israelites tried to persuade their compatriots to make a bond with the heathen, "for since we departed from them we have had much sorrow" (1 Macc. 1:11). Their desire to end the suffering springing from their isolation was met with bitter resistance by the orthodox. Thus the building of an altar at Modein became the signal for the rebellion led by Mattathias and his five sons, which finally developed into the Maccabean War.

Mattathias' own role in the ensuing struggles was small, and the leadership soon passed over to one of his sons, Judas, called Maccabeus. Scholars have oversimplified the problem of this name, which was later adopted by Judas' entire family, by suggesting that the term "Maccabeus" was derived from the Hebrew *maqqab*, meaning "hammer" (cf. the name of Charles Martel). It is at least as probable that

"Maccabeus" was the abbreviation of another name, originally ending in *-jahu*. After Judas' death (161 B.C.), leadership was assumed first by his brother Jonathan, and later (143 B.C.) by his brother Simon, who was given the hereditary title of High Priest. Simon was succeeded by his son John Hyrcanus, in 135 B.C., and later by Aristobulus I (104–103 B.C.), who was proclaimed king, and became the founder of the royal House of Maccabi, or of the Hasmoneans as the Talmud and the Midrash call it. It is difficult to tell what the last name, obviously derived from "Simon," really means. Josephus applied the name of "Hasmon" not only to Mattathias' father, but also to a distant forefather of the Maccabeans. Apparently the Hasmoneans themselves liked to be called Maccabeans, which had become a most honourable title.

Judas Maccabeus exhausted the Seleucid armies by constant guerilla warfare, for which they were not prepared. In 164 B.C., when Antiochus led the main body of his army against the Parthians, Lysias, the governor of the western Seleucid Empire, was forced to open negotiations with the Jews. At first he promised no more than to put in a good word for them, if they, in turn, would agree to become loyal subjects of the King. In March 164 B.C., Antiochus published an edict granting full amnesty to all those who would lay down their arms and return to their homes. He even promised to let them live according to the Law of Moses (cf. 2 Macc. 11). By this edict he put a stop to the persecution of the orthodox Jews, but failed to restore the purity of the temple. This was achieved by Judas Maccabeus himself when he took Jerusalem (but not the Acra) in the Autumn of the same year. Then, on the 25th day of Kislev 164 B.C. the temple was cleansed and rededicated. His victory is commemorated by Jewry during the Hanukah festival, an annual celebration of rekindling the temple lights.

The fruits of this victory were endangered in 163 B.C., when Lysias besieged the Temple Hill. However, at the last moment, he was forced to enter into a new pact with Judas Maccabeus, the text of which is recorded in 2 Macc. 11: 22–30. Menelaus was executed, and Alcimus, of the House of Aaron, was proclaimed High Priest with the approval of the pious. The *status quo ante* had been restored, and Jerusalem was one again governed by a High Priest who, with the support of the Seleucid soldiers, supervised the observance of the Mosaic law. Though the Acra remained it had lost jurisdiction over the Jerusalem *ethnos*. Coexistence was apparently working well once again.

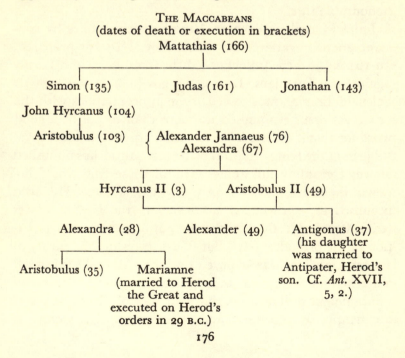

THE MACCABEANS
(dates of death or execution in brackets)
Mattathias (166)

Simon (135)   Judas (161)   Jonathan (143)
John Hyrcanus (104)

Aristobulus (103)   { Alexander Jannaeus (76)
                     { Alexandra (67)

Hyrcanus II (3)   Aristobulus II (49)

Alexandra (28)   Alexander (49)   Antigonus (37)
                                                (his daughter
                                                was married to
Aristobulus (35)   Mariamne   Antipater, Herod's
                    (married to Herod   son. Cf. *Ant.* XVII,
                    the Great and   5, 2.)
                    executed on Herod's
                    orders in 29 B.C.)

XIX

THE MACCABEAN KINGDOM

Coexistence was not, however, accepted by Judas Maccabeus, who continued to harass the Seleucids, and who waited for his hour to strike. He was rewarded on the 13th Adar 161 B.C., when he scored a great victory over a Seleucid army led by Nicanor. This event is remembered by Jewry to this day. A year later, Judas fell in battle. He was succeeded by Jonathan, who fought against the Seleucids for three years, and finally surrendered to them. Having left hostages as a guarantee of his loyalty, Jonathan was allowed to establish a fairly independent government in Michmash (west of Jericho). Jonathan may therefore be considered the real founder of the Maccabean state. It was he who knew how to play off the constant quarrels between the various pretenders to the Seleucid crown, cleverly buying new privileges for money or soldiers, and who, in 150 B.C., allowed himself to be proclaimed High Priest by the usurper Alexander Balas, then engaged in a bitter feud with Demetrius I. Two years later, Jonathan was made general and joint ruler. Later still, when Jonathan sided with Antiochus VI against Demetrius II, he was incarcerated and killed. However, he left his brother Simon heir to a realm that was united within and strong without.

Subsequent generations were to remember Simon's reign as one of great peace and prosperity. Simon managed to secure vast concessions from Demetrius II and to drive out his opponents from the Acra. The fall of this citadel on the 23rd of Iyar was commemorated by an annual festival. 1 Macc. 14 lists the various honours that were bestowed on Simon, not only by the Jews, but by Rome and Sparta as well. In 143 B.C., Simon was solemnly appointed High Priest by the people and the priesthood. The appointment of a man of such lowly birth was most unusual; more remarkable still was that the decree of 141 B.C. should have made this office hereditary. In fact, Simon's heir, John Hyrcanus I, so greatly increased the power and influence of the family, that Aristobulus I had no difficulty in assuming the title of king in 104 B.C. True, this concentration of power and glory did not please all Israel, and many voices were raised amid the general jubilation, warning that the Law of Moses was being endangered. Among those whom Simon had driven out of the Acra were many law-abiding Jews whose orthodoxy caused them to shun all contacts with the worldly rulers of the theocratic state of Judah.

In fact the Maccabeans acted much like other Oriental despots, all of whom tried to enhance their glory by wars of conquest. Thus Simon occupied the Philistine coastal strip and advanced to the Mediterranean, making Jaffa his chief port. John Hyrcanus I captured Edom and Samaria and destroyed the temple of Mt. Gerizim. He also occupied Shechem, Scythopolis and Jezreel. Aristobulus I added Ituraea and Galilee to his empire. Under Alexander Jannaeus (103–76 B.C.) the Maccabeans occupied further coastal regions and also Transjordan, misquoting Biblical texts in order to justify their claims to these territories. The Patriarchs, Judges and Kings were all cited for calling what

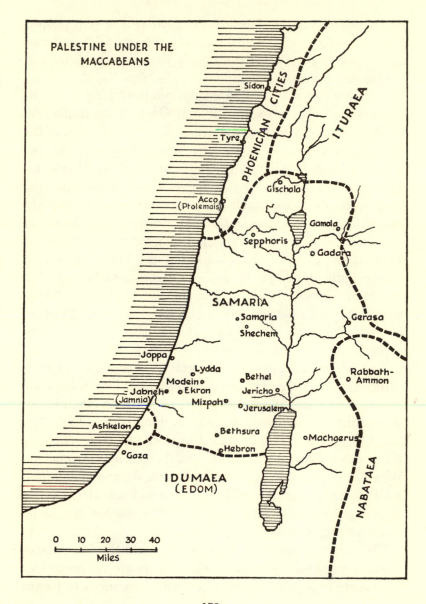

PALESTINE UNDER THE MACCABEANS

Sidon

PHOENICIAN CITIES

ITURAEA

Tyre

Gischala

Acco
(Ptolemais)

Gamala

Sepphoris

Gadara

SAMARIA

Samaria

Shechem

Gerasa

Joppa

Lydda

Bethel

Rabbath-
Ammon

Modein

Ekron

Jericho

Jabneh
(Jamnia)

Mizpah

Jerusalem

Ashkelon

Bethsura

Machaerus

Gaza

Hebron

IDUMAEA
(EDOM)

NABATAEA

0   10   20   30   40

Miles

was open robbery the restoration of God's gift to His people. Even so, there is no doubt that, since the kingdom was once again nearly the size of Solomon's domain, the Jews had reason to feel proud.

Alexander Jannaeus ruled a kingdom stretching from Mt. Carmel in the north to well beyond Gaza in the south. All Galilea, Samaria, Judea, Idumea (with the exception of the small Ashkelon enclave) and much of the desert, now belonged to him, together with Gaulanitis, Gilead, Perea and Moab in Transjordan. Following established precepts, the subject nations were forcibly circumcised and so brought under the Law of Moses. Popular resistance to these and similar measures endangered the inner security of the state. Excavations in Gezer have revealed the foundations of a palace built for Simon by Philistine conscript labour. On one of the stones a labourer had engraved the curse: "May fire destroy Simon's palace." Such feelings were, of course, glossed over by the court historians, and so were the many objections by the Jewish people themselves.

The Maccabeans employed foreign mercenaries in their campaigns, and these men inspired general loathing. They spread Hellenistic ideas wherever they went, and their idiom increasingly crept into the Hebrew language. Originally, Maccabean coins were inscribed in ancient script, reflecting the return to ancient traditions. But then there was a change. Whereas only the king's Hebrew name had appeared at first, a Greek name was now added. Later still, the Greek name appeared before the Hebrew, and finally the Hebrew name was dropped altogether.

The conflict between the pious Jews and the Maccabean rulers reached its climax under the reign of Alexander Jannaeus (103–76 B.C.), whom Josephus mentions at length in *Ant.*, XIII, 13, 3 ff. Alexander not only waged a number of wars (most of which were unsuccessful), but also turned to ocean navigation. This aspect of his reign is borne out, not only by reports about his building activities in Jopé (Jaffa), but also by the presence of anchors on coins issued under his reign. From the Hebrew and Greek inscriptions on these coins we can deduce that Jannaeos was the Greek for Jonathan. His kind of navigation must have been sheer piracy, for the two terms were synonymous under the Seleucids. In fact, two later Maccabeans—Aristobulus II and Hyrcanus II—accused each other of piracy before the Roman general Pompey.

Some military failures notwithstanding, Alexander Jannaeus managed to extend his empire. He was saved from utter destruction at the hands of the Ptolemy of Cyprus by the intervention of Cleopatra, Ptolemy's mother. The Pharisees, too, were bitterly opposed to Jannaeus, as we may gather from the Talmud. They were headed by Rabbi Simeon ben Shetach, who engaged the King in post-prandial arguments. The Pharisees found a ready ear among an ever-growing number of people, who all agreed that a general was not the ideal man to hold the office of High Priest. The Pharisees also argued that his mother had been a slave and that he was thereby disqualified from holding this high office.

During the Feast of the Tabernacles the conflict came to a head, and Alexander was bombarded with ritual lemons, while officiating in the Temple. He retaliated by setting his own mercenaries upon the people, killing 6,000 of them. All his hirelings had been recruited from Pisidia and Cilicia in Asia Minor, and we can imagine that they had no qualms about trampling any resistance of the Jews underfoot.

When, after an unsuccessful campaign, Alexander barely escaped with his life and managed to flee to Jerusalem, he started a civil war lasting six years. He called in his mercenaries from the garrisons of Alexandria and Hyrcanium, where they had their Winter quarters, and set them on the people. Hatred of the tyrant became so intense that the people longed for his death and called for the help of Demetrius, the Seleucid King. Alexander Jannaeus would surely have been killed, had patriotism not dictated at the last moment that a bad Jewish ruler was better than even the best foreigner. Though he carried the day, his evil deeds had undoubtedly destroyed many pious hopes, and awakened new ones in their stead.

The Seleucid Kings

Seleucus I (Da. 11 : 5)	312–282
Antiochus I Soter	282–262
Antiochus II Deus (Da. 11 : 6)	262–246
Seleucus II Callinicus (Da. 11 : 7–9)	246–226
Seleucus III Ceraunus (Da. 11 : 10)	226–223
Antiochus III (the Great) (Da. 11 : 11–18)	223–187
Seleucus IV Philopator (Da. 11 : 20) or Soter (2 Macc. 3 : 1–4 :7)	187–175
Antiochus IV Epiphanes (Da. 11 : 21 ff.)	175–164
Antiochus V Eupator	164–162
Demetrius I Soter	162–150
Alexander Balas	150–145
Demetrius II Nicator	145–138
Antiochus VII Sidetes	138–129
Demetrius II Nicator (2nd time)	129–125
Seleucus V	125
Antiochus VIII Grypus	125–113
Antiochus IX Cyzenicus	113–75

In 83 B.C., the Seleucid Empire fell to Tigranes, King of Armenia, who was driven out by the Romans. Under Roman overlordship, Antiochus Asiaticus continued to reign until 65 B.C.

XX

ROMAN INTERVENTION

THE Maccabean successes and conquests are partially explained by the encouragement and support given to the Jews by a people before whom Jerusalem was to bow down one day—the Romans. For Rome was bent on bringing about the decline of the Hellenistic kingdoms. Antiochus III had felt their sting in the battle of Magnesia (190 B.C.), where they defeated him and forced him to pay a large tribute. Antiochus IV Epiphanes, too, as we have seen, had had a spectacular clash with Rome during his campaign against Egypt. Daniel's apocalyptic vision referred to this event: "At the time appointed he shall return and come into the south; but it shall not be this time. For the ships of Kittim shall come against him, and he shall be afraid and withdraw." (Dan. 11 : 29 ff.). The expression "Kittim" in apocalyptic literature generally refers to the Greeks, though in this case the term is used to describe the Romans, who may well have sailed in Greek ships. From other sources we know that Popilius Laenas, on behalf of the Roman senate, ordered Antiochus IV not to press his claim on Egypt. When Antiochus declared that he would have to consult his "philoi" or "friends," Popilius drew a large circle about the King with his staff and said: "This is where you will make your decision." According to the Book of Daniel, Antiochus then vented his rage upon Jerusalem, a less formidable target.

At that stage, Rome still played the part of an interested spectator, gleefully biding her time. Roman history is unusually silent about this period, and it is only by chance that we learn that the civil war in Egypt was the subject of a discussion in the Roman senate, that Roman merchants and shipbuilders sided with Ptolemy VIII, and that an unofficial deputation was sent to the Orient with orders to keep Rome informed and to establish new contacts. As a result, a pact was signed between Judas Maccabeus and Rome in 161 B.C. Though this pact, which was renewed time and again, stood the Maccabeans in good stead during their struggle against the Seleucids, it eventually became the cause of their downfall, for in 63 B.C. Pompey turned Palestine into a Roman province.

Let us now look at the period of transition from Seleucid to Roman supremacy over Palestine.

The first official contacts between the Jewish people and Rome were made during the reign of the young Seleucid King, Antiochus V Eupator (164–162 B.C.), whose governor and general, Lysias, advanced on Jerusalem with so much self-assurance that a host of slave-traders followed behind him like so many carrion crows. The Roman economy was increasingly dependent on slaves, and the Seleucids must have thought that, by delivering Jews to Rome, they might help to pay the tribute Rome had imposed upon them after the defeat at Magnesia. Lysias, however, though vastly superior to the Jews, was forced to open negotiations with them at the very moment when his victory was certain, no doubt under Roman pressure. The resulting peace treaty gave the Maccabeans breathing space to reorganise their forces, thus helping Rome to weaken the Seleucid Empire, which eventually fell into the legions' lap like a ripe plum. Rome never gave direct military aid to the Jews, and furthered its own ends by a consistent policy of "divide and conquer."

In the Second Book of the Maccabees we find a record of the diplomatic correspondence preceding the peace treaty. It consists of a letter by Lysias to the Jews, two letters by King Antiochus V to Lysias, and a letter by the Roman ambassadors to the Jews. All these documents are dated the 148th year of the Seleucid era, i.e. 165–164 B.C. The Roman ambassadors were Quintus Memmius and Titus Manlius (2 Macc. 11 : 34). The documents differ markedly in tone, for while the Romans' letters were addressed to the Jewish people (*demos*), Lysias wrote to the Jewish *plethos*— a term less respectful. There is no reason to think that 2 Maccabees has not reproduced these letters faithfully.

The temporary peace was shattered a short time later, when new struggles flared up between Lysias and Judas Maccabeus. As a result, Judas sent a deputation to Rome. His victories over Nicanor did not blind Judas or Rome to the real strength of Demetrius I, the capable successor of the young Antiochus V. Judas entered into a pact with Rome, the conditions of which are outlined in 1 Macc. 8 : 23–32, and by Josephus in *Ant.*, XII, 10, 6. Josephus' report was undoubtedly taken from the former work and what discrepancies there are between the two texts arose through errors of translation, first from the Latin into Hebrew and then from the Hebrew into Greek. The Romans clearly treated the Maccabean state as an equal, which must have irked Demetrius, who looked down on the Maccabeans as rabble.

When the Jewish ambassadors returned from Rome, they found that Judas had fallen in the battle of Elasa. Rome sat by with folded hands while the Jewish army was being defeated. Despite this betrayal, Jonathan, Judas' brother and successor, resumed diplomatic relations with Rome. We are told in 1 Macc. 12 : 1, and in Josephus' *Ant.*, VIII, 5, 8, that a second deputation to Rome also visited Sparta and other cities, probably towards the end of Jonathan's reign. At that time, Jonathan, though an ally of Antiochus VI in his struggles against Demetrius II, could not have helped noticing that Tryphon, the regent of Antiochus, treated him with mistrust—hence Jonathan's continued reliance on Rome. If we look at the diplomatic moves of the time in the light of what we know today, we see that the final outcome was a foregone conclusion. For the Maccabeans there were no allies other than Rome to help in the struggle against the Seleucids. However, this very alliance forced the former priest-kings to turn into worldly diplomats and hence to alienate the orthodox. To the eyes of the small but unified circles of pious Jews, the Maccabees practised the very politics which, in similar historical situations, Isaiah and Jeremiah had castigated. By and large, however, the nation was as short-sighted as its leaders and loudly acclaimed successes which were, in fact, signposts to the final defeat. More jubilant still were the Maccabean court historians who suggested that Rome herself, and not the Jews, had asked for a renewal of the former alliance. In support of their claim, they pointed to Rome's glowing reception of Numinius, Simon's ambassador. Probably Rome's enthusiasm was due largely to Simon's gift of "a shield of gold of a thousand pounds" (1 Macc. 15 : 18).

Simon expected Rome not only to support the Jews in his kingdom, but also to protect those living in the diaspora. Accordingly, Rome sent letters to various kings and governments of which one, addressed to King Ptolemy, is quoted in 1 Macc. 15 : 15–24. Similar letters were sent to many other countries and cities, the names of which are reminiscent of those listed in Acts 2 : 9 ff. From them, we learn how widespread were the Jewish communities on the shores of the Mediterranean in Simon's day, and how great Rome's influence was over these regions.

However, as Rome did no more than write letters, the Seleucids continued the struggle against the Maccabeans. Under Antiochus VII Sidetes (138–129 B.C.), the survival of the Jews was once again threatened to such a degree that John Hyrcanus I appealed for direct Roman help. At the time, Rome herself was having grave internal difficulties under the Gracchi, and felt unable to intervene in any way. Thus, Antiochus had an easy task of destroying the walls of Jerusalem, and of imposing heavy burdens on the inhabitants. The walls were probably not restored until after the death of Antiochus.

However, Jewish faith in Rome remained unshaken, for when Antiochus IX (113–75 B.C.) inflicted heavy losses on John Hyrcanus I, Rome was once again appealed to, as we know from one of the many senate decisions reported by Josephus (*Ant.*, XIV, 10, 22). The relevant senate records were headed "Decision of the Citizens of Pergamon," reflecting the fact that Theodorus, the Maccabean ambassador, had called on Pergamon on his way home from Rome, and persuaded the citizens to subscribe to the alliance. The senate decision mentions Hyrcanus and "Antiochus, the son of Antiochus," and while there is no certainty that these names refer to John Hyrcanus I and Antiochus IX, it is only on that assumption that the decision fits in with the other known facts. The Roman senate requested Antiochus to treat the Jews justly as allies of Rome, and in a second decision demanded the return of all Jewish harbours and

towns. Moreover, no one—except Ptolemy, a Roman ally—
was to export any articles from these harbours and towns
without paying tolls to the Maccabean state. The army of
occupation was to be withdrawn from Jaffa.

We have no record about the effect of these decisions on
Antiochus IX. The mention of Ptolemy's name requires
amplification. During the reign of Antiochus IX, the
Ptolemies and the Seleucids had begun to draw closer together, and the Jewish people quite naturally looked upon
this friendship with great misgivings. Rome, too, may well
have feared the new alliance as threatening her own position
in Western Asia, and by granting Ptolemy special privileges,
the Senate may have tried to drive a wedge between the two
powers. Rome probably held that an independent Jewish
nation was a valuable pawn in her own political game, and
for this reason helped John Hyrcanus I to survive his many
military defeats.[1]

[1] For the Roman incursion into the Seleucid Empire, cf. M. S.
Ginsburg: *Rome et la Judée*, Diss., Paris, 1928. See also H. Fuchs: *Der
geistige Widerstand gegen Rom in der Antike*, Basle, 1938.

XXI

THE RULE OF ROME

DURING the first century B.C., Seleucid power waned as a result of intense struggles for the crown. Hence, no renewal of the Judeo-Roman alliance was asked for. In fact, during the reign of Alexandra, the widow of Alexander Jannaeus (76–67 B.C.), her son Aristobulus II felt strong enough to launch a campaign against Damascus. Judah was endangered once again, when Tigranes, King of Armenia, after a successful attack on the Seleucid Empire, decided to march on Jerusalem. Alexandra bought Tigranes off with expensive presents, while Roman legions under Lucullus advanced on the borders of Armenia. That a barbarian King like Tigranes dared to attack the Seleucid Empire shows better than anything else how much Seleucid prestige had shrunk. Thus Pompey was able to harvest the fruit sown by Roman diplomacy for a century, when he deposed the last of the Seleucid kings, Antiochus XIII, without meeting any resistance. A new chapter in the history of Western Asia had begun, and with it a new phase in the relations between Rome and Jerusalem. It did not take the Maccabeans long to realise how high a price they were expected to pay for their independence which, now that the Seleucid Empire was liquidated, no longer served Rome's purposes. Hence the Maccabean dynasty, too, came to an inglorious end.

That end was hastened by a fraternal quarrel. When

Hyrcanus II and Aristobulus II, the sons of Queen Alexandra, failed to settle their respective claims to the Jewish throne, they called on Pompey, thus giving him a legal pretext to occupy their country. Only then did the two parties bury their hatchet and offer combined resistance to Pompey on the Temple Hill. It took the Romans until the Autumn of 63 B.C. to gain complete victory. Twelve thousand Jews are said to have fallen in a battle which was the logical consequence of the pact Jonathan had signed in 161 B.C.

Roman rule fell heavily on the Jewish people in a number of ways. They had to pay a crippling tax, and the coastal cities were taken away from them, together with Scythopolis, Samaria and Marisa. Only one great concession was made to them: Hyrcanus II, though stripped of his crown, was allowed to continue as High Priest. When, however, Aristobulus' son made desperate attempts to oust Hyrcanus, Gabinius, the Roman governor of Syria, took over even internal control of the Jewish state. His division of the country into five districts with the capitals Jerusalem, Gazara (Gezer) and Jericho in Judea; Sepphoris in Galilea, and Amathus in Perea, was to have far-reaching consequences.

Once the Roman governor came out into the open, Hyrcanus' political power proved to be an empty sham. Possibly he was even dismissed from the high priestly office, and became a sort of glorified beadle in the temple. This assumption is borne out by the fact that Julius Caesar had to restore his old office to him, and to re-affirm its hereditary character. Caesar's act was one of many measures calculated to win Jewish support for the Roman cause. Small wonder that Strabo could report that the Jews were grieved when they heard of Caesar's assassination.

The relationship between Hyrcanus II and the Sanhedrin

poses a number of intricate problems, mainly because of the mutilated and abbreviated form of some of the relevant documents quoted by Josephus in *Ant.*, XII, 10. All we know is that Hyrcanus was granted—or had restored to him—the right to collect the temple taxes, and that he was appointed *ethnarch*, i.e. representative of all Jews, both in Jerusalem and in the diaspora. Hence he acted as mediator in all conflicts between the Jews and the Roman authorities, particularly in Egypt, where anti-Semetic outbursts were not uncommon. According to Josephus, Hyrcanus II sent a deputation to Dolabella, governor of Asia, in 43 B.C., to protest against Roman attempts to impose conscription on the Jews. Dolabella proved sympathetic, and wrote accordingly to Ephesus, with express orders to transmit his message to other towns in Asia Minor. Exemption from Roman military service was, however, only a part of a much larger problem, viz. the recognition of Judaism as *religio licita*, and hence of Jewish Sabbath observance.

Next to the High Priest and Ethnarch, a new personage came to the fore at the time—the procurator. The first bearer of this title in Judah was Antipater who, oddly enough, was not a Jew but an Idumean, and hence a member of what had been a subject people of the Jews. In practice, he was Rome's chief deputy and the guardian of Roman interests. Radical changes in the impost system enslaved Jerusalem to Rome as never before, and it was Antipater's main task to supervise the smooth collection and transmission of the taxes.

XXII

THE HOUSE OF HEROD

Although Hyrcanus II was re-appointed High Priest, it soon appeared that the office of *Epitropos* was much more important to the Romans. When Antonius and Octavian had scored their victory at Phillipi (42 B.C.), countless deputations came to pay their respects to Antonius in Bithynia, including a delegation from Judah. The Jews intended to complain that Antipater had delegated too much power to his sons, Herod and Phasael, but according to Josephus (*Ant.*, XIV, 12, 2), Herod was so skilled a diplomat that the Jewish delegation was not even received. For the first time, Jerusalem felt the sting of the man who, though an Idumean by descent, was to enter history as King of the Jews, and who came to be known as "the Great." Most of the events we are about to describe are centred on his person.

Herod enjoyed the confidence of Caesar, of Crassus, of Antonius and of Augustus. In 40 B.C., Herod, in the company of Antonius and Octavian, headed a triumphal procession through the streets of Rome, and was proclaimed King of Judea in the Capitol by the Senate. His subsequent rise overshadowed all the events that preceded his accession to the throne. It was at his behest that Antigonus, Hyrcanus' heir (40–37 B.C.), was beheaded by Antonius, and that the Maccabean House lost its last ruler. Once again, Jerusalem witnessed a blood-bath, as Roman legionaries and Herod's mercenaries streamed into the city (37 B.C.). Though Antigonus had surrendered unconditionally to the Syrian legate, Herod insisted on his death. From 37–34 B.C., Herod tyrannised his subjects in Jerusalem, owing responsibility to no one but the Roman Emperor Augustus, who, according to Mommsen, had a special liking for him. Herod was expected to be a pioneer of Roman culture, and to have his children educated in Rome. He has the right to use the titles of *rex*, *tetrarch* and *dynast*. Members of his house were treated as Roman allies, and were entitled to wage wars of their own, subject to Roman approval. They were also allowed to fight by the side of the Roman legions as auxiliaries, bearing their own standards, and could appoint their own heirs, subject again to Roman approval. Typical representatives of such *reges socii*, apart from Herod himself, were his sons, Archelaus, Herod Antipas and Philippus, who shared their father's kingdom between them, and Herod Agrippa I who, during the years A.D. 37, 40 and 41–44, acted as Roman procurator. All these rulers owed their positions and titles to Rome. After the death of Herod the Great (4 B.C.), their dependence on Rome became even more pronounced, for though Augustus approved Herod's choice of Archelaus as successor, he stripped Archelaus of the crown. Archelaus was simply an ethnarch, who had to share the realm with his brothers, the tetrarchs. None of their titles were hereditary.

Augustus also made use of his right to incorporate parts of the ethnarchy into the Roman province of Syria. In A.D. 6, when a delegation of Jews and Samaritans complained to Rome about the behaviour of Archelaus, who could not refute the charges brought against him, he was banished and his property confiscated by an imperial edict. Nor did Herod

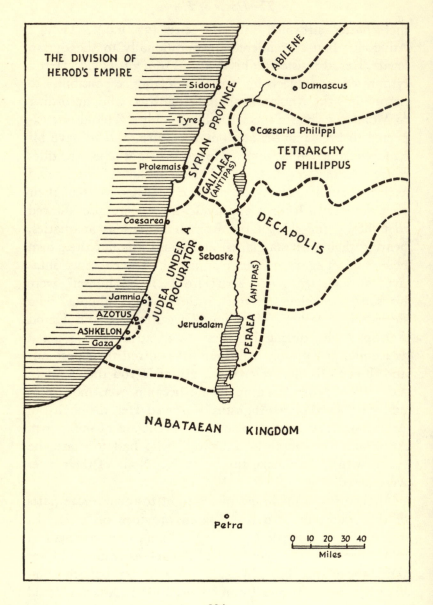

THE DIVISION OF
HEROD'S EMPIRE

ABILENE

Sidon

○ Damascus

SYRIAN PROVINCE

Tyre

○ Caesaria Philippi

Ptolemais

GALILAEA
(ANTIPAS)

TETRARCHY
OF PHILIPPUS

Caesarea

DECAPOLIS

JUDEA UNDER A PROCURATOR

○ Sebaste

Jamnia

PERAEA (ANTIPAS)

AZOTUS

ASHKELON

Jerusalem

Gaza

NABATAEAN   KINGDOM

○ Petra

0 10 20 30 40
Miles

Antipas fare much better when his nephew Agrippa denounced him as an enemy of the Emperor Caligula. Since he could not give a satisfactory explanation why he had been storing up arms, he, too, was sent into exile. Agrippa was ordered to stop work on the walls of Jerusalem because the Roman governor of Syria looked with suspicion on the extensive building operations. Again, when Agrippa, whom no one could have accused of being a Jewish nationalist, summoned a conference of five vassal-kings in Tiberias, the conference was vetoed by the governor of Syria as an unauthorised arrogation of powers. Nevertheless Agrippa managed to remain *tetrarch* until his death (A.D. 44), and so did his brother Philippus (died A.D. 34), simply because they both subordinated their own political interests to those of Rome.

What renown Herod the Great enjoyed among his contemporaries was largely the result of the many buildings he put up. Not only was Jerusalem, his capital, turned into a most impressive city, but other towns were also greatly embellished. The whole of Palestine must have changed its appearance at the time, though of all the many new buildings, the temple and the royal palace in Jerusalem were by far the most imposing. All that has been preserved of the temple is the platform—the *Harām esh Sherīf*, now covered with Islamic shrines, including the Dome of the Rock and the Al Aksa Mosque. The vastness of this platform invariably impresses all visitors to Jerusalem, and so does the solidity of the surrounding walls. The platform covers an area of about 900 × 1,550 feet and is probably one of the largest sacred areas of antiquity. Herod supervised the operation for ten years. After his death the work was continued, though with interruptions. At last, in the year A.D. 64, under Agrippa II,

Herod's project was completed—six years before its destruction.

Nor was it by his temple alone that Herod the "half-Jew" —as he was contemptuously called—showed his respect for the religious traditions of his people. He also erected the holy tombs of the Patriarchs at Hebron, now one of Islam's chief shrines (the *Harām el-Khalil*). The masonry is very similar to that of the temple in Jerusalem. In addition, he had the Sacred oak of Abraham at Mamre surrounded with a wall, later used by Hadrian for defensive purposes. Impressive though all these holy works were, Herod is more famous still for his secular buildings. The royal palace which, from the western hill, overlooked the whole of Jerusalem, was Herod's most impressive monument. The three tall towers on its northern wall were named respectively Hippicus—Herod's friend, Phasael—Herod's brother, and Mariamne—Herod's wife. The "Tower of David" in the modern Arab citadel was probably the base of the Tower of Phasael. From the royal palace, Jerusalem's main street led straight to the temple. Other streets, too, were built in the Graeco-Roman way—straight and intersecting at right angles. On the north-western face of the Temple hill, Herod built the Antonia—a fortress named in honour of Antony— which was reached from the Temple hill by steps. Each of its four tall towers was built like a *migdol*, the traditional bastion of Palestine. Today a tall rock marks the spot on which the Antonia fortress once stood.

Outside Jerusalem, Herod's buildings showed a strong Roman influence. Samaria was extended, embellished and renamed Sebaste (Greek for Augustus), a name which it still bears in Arabicised form. The port of Caesarea was renamed Sebastos Limen. From excavations made in 1931–1933 by an American archaeological expedition led by J. W. Crow-foot, we know what Herod's Samaria must have looked like. Here, on the site of the former palace of the House of Omri, a temple was erected to Augustus in 27 B.C. This submission to the emperor cult is the more remarkable in that it was such a flagrant breach of Jewish law. Five years later, work was begun on a Sebasteion in Caesarea. Among Herod's many other buildings was his Winter palace in Jericho. The palace was surrounded with pools and gardens and boasted an amphitheatre and a hippodrome. Traces of Herod's Jericho are still visible on either side of the Wâdi el Qelt, just where it leaves the mountains.

Despite his great temple, Herod was detested by all the Jews, whose hatred may be gathered by reading the story of Herod's slaughter of the children of Bethlehem (Matt. 2 : 16). The reason why Josephus glossed over this aspect of Herod's life is his reliance for biographical details on Nicholaus of Damascus, who, as we saw, was Herod's secretary and admirer. However, the Talmud describes the disappointment of the Pharisees when they realised what false hopes they had placed in the King. Herod's death—shortly before the Passover in the year 4 B.C.—was greeted with joy.

Across the ages, Herod strikes us as a reckless and often successful gambler. He was a ruthless enemy, an ambitious schemer and a shrewd politician, who used his Roman connections to his own best advantage. His personal bravery and resourcefulness were first revealed when, shortly after his appointment as governor of Galilee (47 B.C.), he attacked the so-called bandit Ezechias. At the time, Herod was reprimanded by the Sanhedrin for having exceeded his orders by killing Ezechias, whom many considered a champion of Jewish freedom. Herod, safe in the knowledge that he enjoyed the protection of the Roman governor of Syria, dismissed the Sanhedrin's complaint in a cavalier manner, and in the end the whole affair had to be hushed up by the weak Hyrcanus II. During Antony's quarrel with Octavian, Herod was sent by Cleopatra to chasten the Nabataean king, who had refused to pay his tribute. This lucky absence saved Herod from having to share his friend Antony's fate.

In 42 B.C. Herod married Mariamne, whose mother, Alexandra, was the daughter of the Hasmonean King Hyrcanus II. In this way he hoped to lend his reign some vestige of legitimacy. When Antigonus was assassinated in 37 B.C., Hyrcanus would have become High Priest, had not his disfigurement—Hyrcanus' ears had been cut off in captivity—made him unacceptable under Jewish law. Herod then appointed Ananel, an unknown man of Egyptian or Babylonian origin, High Priest of Jerusalem. By this action, he fell out with his mother-in-law Alexandra, who considered that her son Aristobulus was the only legitimate candidate for the office. Herod's friends "ducked" the young Aristobulus in a pool in Jericho until he drowned, probably because the citizens of Jerusalem had expressed their liking for Aristobulus during the Feast of the Tabernacle (in 36 or 35 B.C.). One family murder was apparently not enough for Herod, for when his sister Salome incited his jealousy, he accused his wife Mariamne of infidelity and had her killed as well (29 B.C.). A year later, Herod executed Alexandra, Mariamne's mother, against whom he trumped up a charge of treason. Having thus killed off the last of the Hasmoneans, Herod had permanently alienated all those patriots to whom the Maccabean House was the embodiment of Jewish nationalism.

When it suited him, Herod would even offend his Roman

overlords. In 10 B.C. he decided to attack the Arabs without consulting Augustus, who wrote him a sharp note terminating their friendship and advising Herod that he would henceforth be treated as a subject (*Ant.*, XVI, 9, 3). Even so, Herod continued to wear crown, sceptre, purple and diadem, and no Roman legionaries were sent to his country in his lifetime. Herod was allowed to command his own navy and army. His soldiers were mainly non-Jews whose number was regulated from Rome, and who were stationed in military camps near the borders of his territory. Herod had unlimited judicial powers, was entitled to change the criminal code at will and also to pronounce the death sentence, except on those members of the royal family whom Rome might consider as possible future rulers.

He was also empowered to distribute small estates to the *kleroi*, his mercenaries, and large areas including even small towns to his favourites—for instance to Antipater, his son, or to Ptolemy, his chancellor. All taxes were assessed at his whim. His reign was therefore reminiscent of that of the Egyptian Ptolemies about whom extant sources tell us much. Herod appointed all state dignitaries, from the highest to the lowest, unlike Hyrcanus II, over whom Caesar himself set Antipater as governor. It is doubtful whether Herod had the right to mint silver; excavations so far have only brought to light copper coins of a certain type. This was probably no accident, but merely the continuation of an earlier traditions, for the Maccabeans, too, minted nothing but copper coins during their reign.

There is no evidence that, as *rex socius*, Herod held a special position in the Roman Empire; the only special privilege granted to him by Augustus in 22 B.C. and confirmed in 12 B.C. was that he was allowed to appoint his own heir. We know, however, that Herod's wishes were not carried out in all respects.

A glance at the map will show the full extent of Herod's domain—from Damascus in the north right down to Egypt in the south. When Augustus appointed Herod's brother Pheroas ruler over the newly created Transjordan, he probably did so in order to limit Herod's powers. Though Augustus was anxious to protect his turbulent borders with strong men, he did not like them to be too powerful. Even so, Herod was later presented by a grateful Rome with Trachonitis, Batanea and Auranitis, all to the north-east of Lake Galilee.

Along the eastern caravan routes across the Jordan lay Decapolis (Mark 5 : 20; 7 : 31; Matt. 4 : 25). It was an alliance of Greek city states, probably founded under Pompey to protect its inhabitants against the neighbourhood, and formed a bulwark and centre of Graeco-Roman culture. Among the cities in the Decapolis, Pliny the Elder listed: Damascus, Philadelphia, Raphana, Scythopolis, Gadara, Hippos, Dion, Pella, Gerasa and Cantha, some of which are mentioned in the New Testament. The largest of them all, Scythopolis, was west of the River Jordan; all the others lay to the east. The individual cities were not administered by one and the same governor; Damascus, for instance, was part of Syria. Excavations, particularly in Gerasa, have emphasised the Hellenistic character of these cities with their amphitheatres, Greek temples, stadia, etc.

Life in the Decapolis was an illustration of the extent to which Jewish customs and morals had lost their hold. Palestine had become the battleground of two opposed cultures, and though the Jews did not surrender voluntarily (in *Ant.*, XVII, 2, 4, Josephus reports that Pheroas' wife supported the Pharisees' refusal to swear allegiance to Augustus), there is no doubt that Roman manners were gaining much ground towards the end of Herod's reign.

To explain why the Messiah, though born in Bethlehem, grew up in Nazareth, St. Matthew tells us that Joseph moved his household when he heard that Archelaus had succeeded Herod, his father, as King of Judea (Matt. 2 : 22). In fact, this most unpopular of Herod's sons was proclaimed ethnarch and not king. The New Testament tells us nothing more about him since, after a complaint by the elders of Jerusalem and Samaria, he was probably banished to Gaul in the year A.D. 6. On the other hand, the New Testament contains six references to Herod Antipas, tetrarch over Galilee and Perea, two regions divided from each other by Samaria and Decapolis. Jesus had a poor opinion of this Herod, whom He called a fox (Luke 13 : 32). It was Herod Antipas who beheaded John the Baptist when John declared the King's marriage to Herodias, Herod's sister-in-law, unlawful (Mark 6 : 14–29; Matt. 14 : 1–12; cf. Luke 3 : 19 ff.; 9 : 7–9). In the story of the Passion, the name of Herod Antipas is coupled with that of Pilate, for, according to Luke 23 : 7–12, Herod's former enmity towards the Roman governor had turned into friendship.

Herod Antipas enjoyed the protection of Tiberius (A.D. 14–37) in whose honour he named his newly built Tiberias. At first many Jews refused to live there ostensibly because its site had been a cemetery, but later they must have changed their minds, for Tiberias became a centre of rabbinical learning. The death of the Emperor Tiberius led to the downfall of Herod Antipas. The new Roman Emperor, Caligula (A.D. 31–41), was a friend of Herodias' brother Agrippa, who lived in Rome and whom he appointed tetrarch and king. We know that the citizens of Alexandria rioted when Agrippa passed through on the way to his new kingdom. An effigy of the King was carried through the streets to the accompaniment of derisive shouts of *Maran* (Lord!). Herod Antipas, too, was enraged when he heard that Agrippa, a notorious spendthrift and adventurer, whom only a short while ago he had demoted to *agoranomos* (market supervisor) was now his superior. In the company of his wife Herodias, he went to complain to Caligula, only to be met by counter-accusations which led to his being banished to Gaul. Herod's tetrarchy was handed over to Agrippa, whose name we meet again in the Acts of the Apostles.

Philippus, the third son of Herod the Great, became tetrarch of Ituraea and Trachonitis (Luke 3 : 1); according to Josephus he also ruled over Batanaea, Auranitis, Gaulanitis and Panias, which had small Jewish populations. He married Salome, Herodias' daughter, and built the city of Caesarea Philippi mentioned in Matt. 16 : 13 and Mark 8 : 27. Philippus was the first Jewish ruler to mint coins bearing the likeness of the Roman Emperor. After his death (A.D. 34), his tetrarchy was first incorporated into the Roman province of Syria, and three years later proclaimed a kingdom and presented to Agrippa.

XXIII

THE FIRST WAR AGAINST ROME

MEANWHILE Archelaus' ethnarchy, comprising Judea, Samaria, and Idumea, had been handed over to Roman procurators. Their names were: Coponius (A.D. 6–9), Marcus Ambibulus (9–12), Annius Rufus (12–15), Valerius Gratus (15–26), Pontius Pilate (26–36), Marcellus (36–37), and Marullus (37–41). While the pious in Jerusalem bore this situation with patient resignation, patriotic Jews found it intolerable and rose up under a certain Judas in Galilee. According to Gamaliel the Pharisee, this Judas appeared in the days of the census (ordered by Quirinus in A.D. 7), had the support of many people, and then perished (Acts 5:37). He was the spokesman rather than the founder of the party of zealots, which also included Simon, Jesus' disciple. In the vanguard of the zealots were the Sicerians (dagger-bearers), who were to play a leading part in the subsequent war against Rome.

When Jesus began His ministry, Judea was governed by Pontius Pilate, the only Roman procurator about whom we are informed to any extent. Theoretically he was subject only to Rome, but in practice he was subordinate to the governor of Syria. Thus we know that Vitellius, the Syrian legate, ordered Pilate to Rome in 36, to explain why he had suppressed the Samaritan rebellion so brutally. Pilate left the collection of taxes in the hands of the Sanhedrin, who employed "publicans" for the purpose. The taxes went into the *fiscus*, the royal treasury, and Jesus' "Render to Caesar the things that are Caesar's" (Matt. 22 : 21) referred to this very matter.

It is very difficult to decide to what extent the Sanhedrin was allowed to pass sentences of death. In their discussion of the Jewish case against Jesus, scholars have come up against this problem time and again, and we shall therefore mention it briefly. The legal procedure described in the Gospel runs counter to relevant passages in the Talmud, from which it is clear that a Jewish court could not possibly have sat at night or come to a decision after a single session, nor could that decision have been made in the house of the High Priest Caiaphas. In addition, according to Matt. 26 : 17, the court sat on the first day of the Passover, a holy day on which legal proceedings were not held. Though these questions do not seem to bear on the problem of the Sanhedrin's jurisdiction, they are in fact very closely connected with it. It must be remembered that the religious views of the Talmud were dictated by the Pharisees, although the Sanhedrin, at least in Jesus' day, was still controlled by the Sadducees. From Josephus we know that the Pharisees and the Sadducees differed widely on legal matters, and that the Sadducees were the stricter of the two in living up to the letter of Old Testament law (*Ant.*, XIII, 10, 6, and XX, 9, 1). Even so, it was generally accepted that extraordinary circumstances required extraordinary steps. Hence it is quite possible that, for the sake of the law, the law was occasionally ignored, and that a court might have sat even during the Passover.

Now, according to John 18 : 31, the Jews were not allowed to sentence any man, while, according to Acts 7 : 58, they stoned Stephen to death. This apparent contradiction is explained by the fact that Stephen was stoned by the populace, while the case against Jesus was presented with all the trimmings of legality. What then was the respective role of the Sanhedrin and Pilate in pronouncing death sentences? We know that the Sanhedrin had the right to pass sentence of death, for Greek inscriptions outside the forecourt of Herod's temple threatened trespassers with execution. Pilate was probably entitled to veto any such sentence, and to pass sentences of death himself when the safety of Rome was involved. This is probably the reason why the Sanhedrin based its case against Jesus on His alleged anti-Roman attitude, thus misrepresenting the spiritual as a political Messiah. However, in that case, it seems strange that the Romans were not asked to pass the sentence themselves, as they were in the case of a hypo-chondriac who kept wailing over the fate of Jerusalem (*Jewish War*, VI, 5, 3). The special treatment of Jesus is further proof that the case against Him was unusual, and that His judges wished to use it as a public warning, with the full semblance of legality.

We gain the impression that Pilate was lacking in tact and strength of purpose. In his *Legatio ad Gaium* (A.D. 38) Philo tells us that Herod Agrippa had a highly unfavourable opinion of the Roman procurator.[1] According to Josephus, he had imperial images brought into Jerusalem under cover of night but removed them again when it became clear that the Jews would rather die than suffer this abomination. Pilate resided at Caesarea, and only during the high festivals did he move to Herod's palace in Jerusalem. Here, too,

[1] E. Lohse: "Die Römischen Statthalter in Jerusalem," *ZDPV*, 74, 1958, pp. 69–78.

he was forced to remove the golden shields bearing his Emperor's image. On another occasion he outraged the people by proposing that the temple treasure be used to pay for an aqueduct. It is against this background that we must read stories like that of the Galileans whose blood Pilate mingled with their sacrifices (Luke 13 : 1).

In judging Pilate, we must bear in mind Palestine's strategic importance to the Roman Empire. In the south and south-east, Palestine bordered on the Nabataean kingdom and in the north-east it was close to the unvanquished Parthian Empire. Rome had to do its utmost to keep the peace in this danger spot, and to stamp out any traces of resistance. Thus Pilate could not afford to ignore the Sanhedrin's accusation against Jesus that they found Him "perverting our nation and forbidding us to give tribute to Caesar, saying that he himself is Christ a king" (Luke 23 : 2).

Pilate's domain was oddly constituted. It contained a large number of enclaves: Gaza, for instance, belonged to Syria, while Ashkelon was an independent city republic in the Greek manner. Jamnia and Azotus were free cities; Phasaelis and Archelais, which had been presented by Herod the Great to his sister Salome, were later bequeathed by her to Livia the wife of Augustus. After Livia's death the cities came into the possession of Tiberius, who appointed special officials over them. As far as we can tell from the Gospels, Jesus made his appearance in the predominantly Jewish areas, and generally avoided those in which the Graeco-Roman influence was strongest.

Pontius Pilate was succeeded as procurator by Marcellus. Soon afterwards, Herod Agrippa I took advantage of Caligula's madness and of Claudius' weakness to obtain and keep the kingship of Judea. His kingdom was larger even than that of Herod the Great, for he even received control of Abilene in Syria. He reigned from A.D. 41–44, during which time he seems to have satisfied Jewish patriots and religious zealots alike. Agrippa was the grandson of Mariamne, and hence could be called an offshoot of the glorious Hasmonean House. By adhering strictly to the Jewish faith he won over the Pharisees, who must have approved of his persecution of the early Christians (Acts 12 : 1 ff.). His friendship with Caligula enabled him on more than one occasion to protect his people's interests. Thus, when the Jews of Jamnia destroyed an altar dedicated to the Emperor and Caligula ordered his image to be set up in the temple of Jerusalem as a punishment, Agrippa persuaded him to change his mind. By contrast, Petronius, governor of Syria, who was responsible for implementing Caligula's order, was summarily told to kill himself when he tried to postpone the erection of the idol and pleaded for the Jews. It was only because Caligula himself was murdered soon afterwards, that Petronius could ignore the order.

Herod Agrippa I is praised in the Talmud and by Josephus for his piety, but did not gain Roman confidence. The Emperor Claudius, immediately upon Agrippa's death (A.D. 44), restored provincial status to Judea. The manner of Agrippa's death is described in Acts 12 : 19–23 and also in *Ant.*, XIX, 8, 2, which differ in only a few details.

Once again it was the time of procurators: Cuspius Fadus (44–46), Tiberius Alexander (46–48), Ventidius Cumanus (48–52), Antonius Felix (52–60), Porcius Festus (60–62), Albinus (62–64) and Gessius Florus (64–66). All these procurators came up against Jewish rebels, the forerunners of the great uprising in A.D. 66.

We must look more closely at two of the procurators

because of their mention in the Book of Acts in the story of the Apostle Paul: Antonius Felix and Porcius Festus. Felix was the husband of Drusilla, who was a daughter of Agrippa I, and formerly the wife of Azizos, King of Emesa. During Felix's reign, the High Priest Jonathan was murdered by the Sicarians, and rumour had it that the assassins were in the procurator's pay. The Book of Acts states that Paul was accused of being an Egyptian Jew who stirred up a revolt and who led 4,000 assassins out into the wilderness (Acts 21 : 38; cf. *Ant.*, XX, 8, 5). The appearance of "assassins" is typical of a time in which apocalyptic and Messianic hopes were being voiced everywhere. The prompt Roman efforts to stamp out the leaders—mass executions were the order of the day—went a long way towards making the people even more rebellious. Since Felix's procuratorship (52–60) overlapped the reign of King Nero (54–68) no gestures of reconciliation could be expected from Rome.

It was to Felix that the Apostle Paul was delivered by the Jews (Acts 23 : 24), and it was he who kept Paul imprisoned, perhaps to please the High Priest, but more probably for ransom. Felix's successor Festus dealt with Paul's case soon after he assumed office in Jerusalem, examining him in the presence of Herod Agrippa II and of Herod's sister Berenice, the widow of Herod of Chalcis, who, according to Josephus (*Ant.*, XX, 7, 3), had a very bad reputation.

Herod Agrippa II was the son of Agrippa I, King of Judea. When his father died, Agrippa II was still a minor and could not ascend the throne. In A.D. 50, however, he was made King of Chalcis, north of Abilene. Three years later, he became King not only of Philip's former tetrarchy but also of Abilene. Nero later conferred on him Tarichea and Tiberias in Galilee, and Abila and Julias in Perea.

Agrippa II managed to preserve his territory until his death (A.D. 93), thanks largely to his pronounced pro-Roman views. His relationship with the priesthood in Jerusalem was bad; we are told that he spied on them from a high tower in his palace, whereupon the priests built a high wall to protect their privacy. The King never tired of preaching that all resistance against Rome was futile (*Jewish War*, XI, 14, 6).

The Zealot rebellion broke out during the administration of Gessius Florus, who had turned a deaf ear to complaints that the Romans were abusing their privileges in a manner calculated to offend the religious susceptibilities of the Jews. Jerusalem remained quiet until Eleazar gave the signal for rebellion by his public refusal to sacrifice to Nero. Meanwhile the Roman fort of Masada (on the western shores of the Dead Sea) had fallen to the rebels, who had killed all the Roman soldiers in it. Despite these events, the Jewish leaders in Jerusalem—Saducees, Pharisees and the supporters of the House of Herod—continued their efforts to patch up the quarrel between the Zealots and Rome, with little support from Herod Agrippa II and no help at all from Gessius Florus. In the end they had to flee to Herod's palace, for the Zealots had already advanced to the Antonia fort. The Romans were defeated and slain, and the Jewish dignitaries, though allowed to leave Herod's palace, were stripped of all their dignities. Though the rebel's cause was greatly weakened by differences between Jerusalem and the provinces, it eventually took the whole country by storm. Wherever the Jews were in the majority, the Roman garrisons were overpowered or driven out, elsewhere the Romans turned the tables on them. Anti-Jewish massacres occurred in Caesarea, Ashkelon, Scythopolis, Damascus and

Alexandria, where the age-old hatred of the Hellenists for the Jews was at last brought out into the open. Only in Herod Agrippa's kingdom was peace preserved completely.

The rebels scored a great victory when they forced Cestias Gallus to call off his siege of Jerusalem in A.D. 66, and inflicted a decisive defeat on his retreating army near Beth Horon. Now, all the rebel bands joined together and even Josephus, then governor of Galilee, made common cause with them. His *Jewish War* is our most important source of all the ensuing events, for it describes the many conflicts in the Jewish camp which were probably responsible for Rome's final victory. Nero's general Vespasian, a brave and able commander, captured Galilee in A.D. 67, and forced the leader of the Zealots, John of Gischala, to flee to Jerusalem where—according to Josephus, at least—he unleashed a reign of terror. All those who strove for a compromise with Rome were slain. After Nero's death (A.D. 68), when there was a struggle for power between Galba, Otho and Vitellius and confusion reigned in Rome, Vespasian had high hopes of being made emperor. From Josephus' report that he was rewarded for having prophesied that Vespasian would rule over Rome, we may take it that the general's eyes were on greater conquests than Palestine. Thus Simon Bar Giora, another Zealot leader, was able to take advantage of Vespasian's preoccupation when he seized Idumea, and came to Jerusalem at the invitation of John of Gischala's enemies. When he arrived, in A.D. 69, a second blood-bath was started. Josephus complains bitterly that the city was now ground between the teeth of two hateful tyrants.

Meanwhile Vespasian reoccupied most of Palestine. In the Summer of 69, he left for Rome because the legions had at last proclaimed him emperor. He handed his command to his son Titus, with express orders to take Jerusalem, Herodium, Masada and Machaerus, the remaining rebel strongholds. The siege of Jerusalem lasted from April to August 70; four legions and many auxiliary troops were thrown into the battle. The first Roman soldiers marched into the city on the 9th day of Ab, a day of mourning observed by Jewry to this day. Hunger played a large part in the Jewish defeat, for three granaries had gone up in flames as a result of the quarrels between Eleazar, a new leader, and John of Gischala. The Jews made a last-ditch stand in Herod's palace where they held out for a month longer, but by September of 70 the whole of Jerusalem with the exception of three towers of Herod's palace was razed to the ground. The temple, too, had been destroyed. However, when Titus entered Rome in triumph in 71, proudly displaying the temple-scrolls, all Palestine had not yet been "pacified." True, Lucilius Bassus, governor of Judea, had an easy task of capturing the Herodium, but Machaerus fell only after a long siege. The fortress of Masada held out until 73, by which time Flavius Silva had become governor of Judea. All the defenders committed suicide.

The outcome of the war in Palestine had far-reaching consequences for Jewry throughout the world. Their religious centre was destroyed, pilgrims could no longer journey to the holy city during the high festivals, and the temple tax of two drachmas had henceforth to be paid to the temple of Jupiter Capitolinus, at least until the Emperor Nerva (96–98) put a stop to this humiliating practice.

XXIV

BAR COCHBA

WE know little about the conditions of the inhabitants of Palestine after the destruction of Jerusalem. From isolated references in the Talmud collected by A. Büchler it appears that relatively few strangers came to settle in Palestine, which had been proclaimed Vespasian's personal property. Leading Jews who had fled before the uprising were allowed to return and to reclaim their possessions. Those who had been imprisoned by the Zealots as friends of Rome were granted special privileges by Titus. Oppressive taxes were imposed on the rest of the Jewish people; the tithe was increased to one-fifth of the harvest. Bands of robbers roamed about the country. Even so, Jewish culture underwent a surprising renaissance, due mainly to the leadership of Rabbi Johanan ben Zakkai.

The blow of the destruction of the temple was softened by the existence of the synagogue which, by concentration on the Holy Scriptures and their interpretation, moulded Judaism in a new stamp, both in Palestine and also in the diaspora. Rabbi Johanan ben Zakkai, who had fled from Jerusalem before the siege, was allowed by Titus to found a school for Torah studies in Jamnia (or Yabneh) south of Jaffa. Thus it came about that the Roman leader and later emperor who had destroyed Israel's national existence and the temple, was responsible for the formation of a new type of Judaism that was to outlive the Roman Empire for many centuries. The *Beth Din* (House of the Law) at Jamnia was the direct successor of the Sanhedrin, and laid the foundations of modern Jewish orthodoxy.

A considerable number of Jews had settled in Mediterranean countries; Philo reports that Alexandria alone had a Jewish population of one million. Uprisings against Roman rule and conflicts with the local population were frequent. In A.D. 73, Vespasian was forced to close the Onias temple in Leontopolis (Egypt) as a possible focus of insurrection. Uprisings also took place under Trajan (115–117), starting in Egypt and Cyrenaica and spreading to Cyprus and even to Mesopotamia. They were extremely serious and the greatest of all occurred in the years 132–135. Some historians have explained that it was caused by Hadrian's edict against circumcision, which was not a specifically anti-Jewish measure since the Jews were not the only ones who circumcised. Dio Cassius, however, our most important source for the events, suggests that the rebellion was set off by Hadrian's decision to rebuild Jerusalem as the *Aelia Capitolina* and to construct a temple to Jupiter Capitolinus on Mt. Zion.

The uprising was led by a Simon called "Bar Cochba" (Aramaic, "son of the star") because Rabbi Akiba had proclaimed him the Star out of Jacob who, by the promise of Num. 24 : 17, would arise as Israel's saviour.[1] (Rabbi Akiba's behaviour, one may note, was quite out of line with the general Rabbinic attitude of remaining aloof from the

---

[1] The documents dealing with Bar Cochba have all been collected by S. Yeivin in the Hebrew work *Bar Cochba's War*, Jerusalem, 1952. In 1960 archaeologists, led by Y. Yadin, discovered eleven further letters dictated by Bar Cochba and written in Greek and Aramaic on papyrus and wood.

struggle with Rome.) Dio Cassius tells us that the Roman legions were hard pressed by the rebels, who hid in caves and rocks, and attacked in isolated groups. In the end, the Emperor Hadrian himself had to appear on the battlefield. Julius Severus was recalled from Britain, and charged with suppressing the rebels at any cost. His men combed cave after cave, and rock after rock, until none of the rebels was left.

Documents unearthed in the Wadi Murabba'at caves mirror this phase of the struggle.[1] Among them is a letter by Bar Cochba to Jeshua ben Gilgula, the local commander of the rebel army. This letter is of great interest, because it gives us Bar Cochba's real name: *Simeon ben Koseba*, thus refuting the assumption that his name was Simeon ben Koziba (as he is called in Rabbinic sources) and supposedly meaning "Simeon, the son of a liar"—a name he is unlikely to have applied to himself. The letter refers to the Galileans, a name which Simon may well have used for the Christians (cf. Acts 1 : 10), thus posing anew the old problem of whether the Christians took part in the uprising against Rome. According to Eusebius (early fourth century) they had not participated in the earlier war and had fled to Pella,[2] sharing the view of many Jews and of Josephus in

[1] The text of the documents was first published (with a commentary) by R. de Vaux, "Quelques textes hébreux de Murabba 'at," and by J. T. Milik, "Une lettre de Siméon Bar Kokheba," *Revue Biblique*, 1953, pp. 268–294. Cf. I. Rabinowitz and H. L. Ginsberg, *BASOR*, 131, 1953, pp. 21–27.

[2] Cf. Eusebius III, 5: "Also the congregation of Jerusalem received, by a prophecy to the leading men among them, orders to leave the city before the war, and to go to a city in Perea, Pella by name. Here those of Jerusalem who believed in Christ lived together, so that God's judgement fell only on those who had done so much evil to Christ and His Apostles." According to Eusebius, God's judgement, proclaimed forty

particular, that resistance to Rome was futile. Hence they were unlikely to have joined the second rebellion, and it seems strange that Bar Cochba's letter does not attack them for their aloofness. Many of his other letters were full of threats and mention, *inter alia*, that he had put one Ben Afluel in chains. Another letter, ostensibly a safe-conduct issued to a shepherd, was, in fact, a report of enemy troop movements. The caves of Murabba'at, too, were finally captured by the Romans. From the damage done to the Torah scrolls and to the phylacteries we may gather with what fury the Romans went to work. Coins with the inscription "on the liberation of Jerusalem" suggest that Bar Cochba was able to occupy the city for a short while. After three-and-a-half years the die was cast. Bether, the last rebel stronghold, fell, and Rabbi Akiba died a martyr's death. Jerusalem was proclaimed the capital of the *Colonia Aelia Capitolina*. A death penalty was proclaimed on all Jews entering the city, and it was not until the fourth century that they were allowed to visit the Wailing Wall on the 9th of Ab of every year, to bemoan the loss of Jerusalem.

On Temple hill, the Romans built a shrine to Jupiter Capitolinus and, from coins minted at Aelia under Hadrian, we know that they dedicated another temple to Venus. Roman streets were built, altering the face of the city, and seven quarters of Jerusalem were occupied by Greeks. Thermal baths, theatres and circuses sprang up.

With the collapse of the revolt of A.D. 135, Israel ceased to be a nation for over eighteen centuries. It was not until

---

years earlier in Luke 21 : 5–38, was fulfilled in A.D. 70. Eusebius' main source was Josephus' *Jewish War*. For a critical view of Eusebius' presentation see S. G. F. Brandon: *The Fall of Jerusalem and the Christian Church*, London, 1951.

14 May 1949, that the country again saw a Jewish state established in the Jewish homeland.

As one contemplates this history of survival one is moved to consider it in the light in which it was already seen at an earlier juncture by the author of the 106th Psalm:

> *Many times he delivered them, but they*
> *were rebellious in their purposes,*
> *and were brought low through their*
> *iniquity.*
> *Nevertheless he regarded their distress,*
> *when he heard their cry.*
> *He remembered for their sake his covenant,*
> *and relented according to the*
> *abundance of his steadfast love.*
> *He caused them to be pitied by all those*
> *who held them captive. . . .*
> *Blessed be the* LORD, *the God, of Israel,*
> *From everlasting to everlasting!*
> *And let all the people say, "Amen!*
> *Praise the* LORD*!"*

TEXTS QUOTED

Index

Index

Index

Index

Index

AUTHORS QUOTED